The Caravan Moves On

The Caravan Moves On

IRFAN ORGA

Dogs bark but the caravan moves on.
OLD TURKISH PROVERB

ELAND
London
2002

First published by Martin Secker & Warburg in 1958

This edition published by Eland Publishing Limited
61 Exmouth Market, London EC1R 4QL in 2002

ISBN 0 907871 97 6

Cover designed by Robert Dalrymple
Cover image © Getty Images
Map drawn by Ateş D'Arcy-Orga

Text set in Great Britain by Antony Gray and
printed in Spain by GraphyCems, Navarra

For Margarete and Ateş, with love
I.O., 1958

For Isabelle and Guillaume, with love
A.O., 2002

Contents

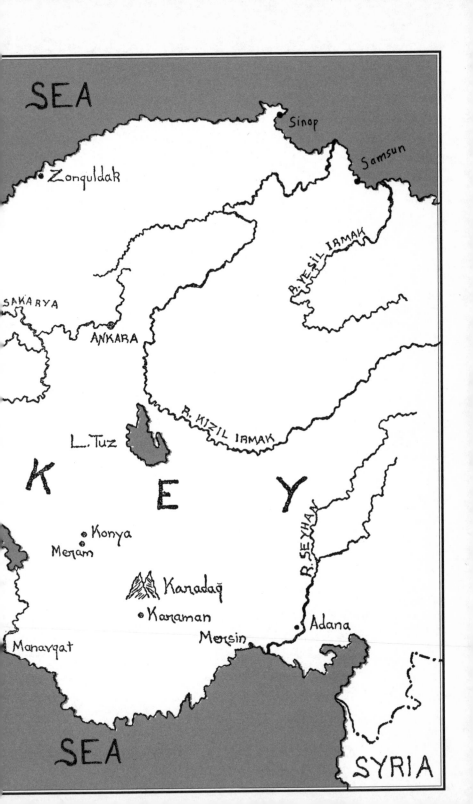

1

Izmir – Family Reunion – The Tame Communist –
The Youth of Smyrna

THE AEGEAN SEA sparkled and, from the shore, windows winked in the sun. Izmir came closer, a toy city of white houses and new concrete wharves. The boat heaved gently, creaking. The glare from the noonday sun was intense, burning my eyes even behind dark glasses.

There was a smell of salt in the air, and something tangyer, lemon trees perhaps. The seagulls swooped, cruel-beaked, low over the water. A gannet cruised on long wings, dazzlingly white where the sun caught the downy underbelly. It fell suddenly, like an arrowhead, sending up a tall shower of spray as it plunged into the sea after fish.

In the foreground the peak of Kadife Kale rose mistily, heat hazed, the shifting shadows violet coloured and tenuous as spun sugar. Farther back, the undulating curves of Manisa Daği were like pale watered silk, their peaks growing less and less substantial as they climbed to the brazen sky.

Passengers began to crowd the rails, their suitcases, wicker baskets and other belongings dumped beside them, so that to step back was to be in danger of breaking one's leg.

It was hot. We all complained of the heat, resenting its invisible presence. We mopped our steaming faces, loosened our too civilised ties, discarded our jackets and commiserated with each other's discomfort. We sailed close inshore, the wake widening out behind us like quicksilver broken into little drops by the eddying waves. Sickened by the smell of sweat mixed with stale perfume, I took my small case and went under the captain's bridge where it was shadier but just as hot. With the aid of binoculars I watched the city coming closer. On Inciraltı Plage a few people lay about in swimming suits. There was a casino with a bright striped awning. Shifting my gaze I saw the hangars of the old sea–planes, and felt a surge of nostalgia for my youth that was gone. I had once spent two feverish years there. I looked at Güzelyalı, where the villas and summer residences of the rich stood in large gardens and the sea washed their lower windows, so close were they built to the shore. On the opposite side was Karşıyaka, my destination. In Karşıyaka the houses stood well away from the sea, yet in summer the spray flung itself against the windows and in winter metal fastenings became brown with salt.

The boat was nearly in and I put away my binoculars, leaning over the rail as we turned before docking, the water foaming madly under the propellers. The harbour was full of fishing boats. Greek, American, Swedish and British flags hung limply in the heat, and on shore lorries were unloaded by sweating men in their vests.

A group of people had assembled to watch us dock. Greetings were called, handkerchiefs waved and I searched for my brother, Mehmet, catching sight of him at last seated on a crate of dried fruit. His eyes caught mine and we waved laconically. His first words after I had dis-embarked were: 'My God, haven't you got fat!' to which I agreed sadly, noting his own slender elegance.

His young son, Kaya, was waiting for us in the car which was parked in the main street. In the back of the car lolled an enormous Afghan hound who bared his teeth when he saw me but fawned over Mehmet. I said very firmly that I would sit in the front and pushed Kaya into the back with the dog, who made a great fuss of the boy but growled every time he caught my eye.

Driving out to Karşıyaka my first impression of changed Izmir was of light and too much open space. The main boulevard was too wide for the numerous small shops. There were public gardens everywhere, the bright flowers drooping wretchedly and only the lush palms revelling in the almost tropical heat. We passed a statue of Kemal Atatürk – something that was to become an inevitable part of one's wanderings across the country, as familiar as a landmark. His memorial in Izmir showed him stern of face, implacable, his hands pointing seawards. Certainly the new wide white Izmir would have been after his own heart. A vast building, nearing completion, was, so Mehmet told me, a hotel which would house two hundred and fifty people. It was to be all chrome and plush, luscious introduction to the Aegean for rich Americans.

The heat was intense. The glare burned the eyes and the sea glittered like a gigantic sunburst of diamonds. The leaves of the city trees hung like green rags, weighed down by the intolerable burden of the heat. Mehmet opened all the windows, remarking: 'In about an hour's time it will be a little better. At one o'clock *inbat* will come' – looking at me anxiously to see if after ten years I still remembered *inbat*, that westerly sea wind which is the breath of life to the people of Izmir.

We ran along the *kordon* and the sea seemed to shine like a vast mirror, reflecting light whitely, bleaching the pastel-tinted houses.

I think, that first morning, I was struck by the brightness of everything, by the cleanliness, the elegant little villas and the purple bougainvillaea that flung itself luxuriantly across garden walls, about public gardens and over the façades of old houses. The scene was un-Turkish. It had wit and gaiety. It was hot and Mediterranean. Furthermore, there was an absence of mosques. There was an air of sun-washed expectancy, and a flaunting lewdness that was enchanting and wholly Levantine. Reconstruction and demolition seemed to be going on in about equal proportions. Marble-faced blocks of flats stood eyeless, facing the sea. A new port was under construction, which would benefit the export trade. Here and there, villas stood raw and new in weedy gardens. In one street a whole row of old houses was being pulled down.

Used to living in the restricted space of a London flat, I found Mehmet's house too large for me. It was all doors and windows, and immense balconies fretted the front of the house in fussy ornamentation.

Crossing what appeared to be an illimitable ocean of polished floor, I was met at about halfway point by my sister-in-law, Bedia, and meeting her again was like coming face to face with a ghost, for the girl I remembered was only palely discernible in her large blue eyes. I was horrified to see the streaks of grey in her hair, although I had long grown used to my own. I dare say I was as much of a shock to her, although she was far too cool to make a personal remark.

My seventeen-year-old niece, Oya, greeted me with a formality I found charming. Kissing my outstretched hand she seemed a stranger; offering me *bon-bons* and orange liqueur she stood before me with downcast eyes, betraying only by an upward flicker of her eyelids that my scrutiny was embarrassing her.

Lunch was served on a balcony filled with flowering plants. As the meal proceeded, and small talk petered out, I discovered I had nothing in common with them. This made me feel superior and self-conscious. They talked for the most part about times past, believing, I think, that this would please me. They resurrected the dead, or spoke of people I had never known. Despite their smattering of culture they knew nothing of life outside Turkey, except what the flaring banners of their newspapers told them. They were as superbly indifferent to world events, to world conferences, as any mountain tribe. The might of the hydrogen bomb passed them by. Time, save in such instances as getting the children off to school or Mehmet to the Naval Hospital, where he was a surgeon-commander, did not govern them. I was continually embarrassed in trying to find some subject of mutual interest. They were indifferent readers, and the books I saw in the house were either medical, printed in French and German, or earthy Turkish novels, products of newly literate Anatolian authors. I tried to talk about these, but it was obvious that they thought I was being rather precious and chi-chi. Bedia remarked distantly that she read for pleasure. It would bore her, she said, to dissect what she was reading while she was reading it and afterwards it usually wasn't worth while. There were so many other things.

My brother's strict Muslim habits forbade him to drink wines or spirits so we drank each other's health in lime juice, freshly extracted from garden produce, and this had a depressive effect upon me. For although I am not what could be called a drinker, I have always found it very pleasant to drink a glass of wine with my meals.

My sister-in-law's thickened figure reminded me of lost youth, and when the conversation turned to my niece's recent betrothal, I wondered what future could be expected for an immature girl married to a young lawyer in a backwater like Izmir. Her serene face, however, and her pertinent remarks assured me she knew what she was doing. She brushed aside the greater freedom of European girls.

'They will grow old and die just the same,' she said contemptuously.

After I had unpacked my one small bag I wondered what to do next. Afternoon quiet invaded the house. Mehmet had returned to the hospital and time was my own for the first time for many years. I found I didn't know what to do with such freedom. Once I peered through the window and saw Bedia sitting on the terrace talking in whispers to a woman who appeared to be wearing an extraordinary hat. Hovering on the edge of boredom, I took off most of my clothes and went to sleep. The sound of soft giggling awoke me, and I sat up to find Kaya huddled at the bottom of the bed regarding me intently.

'You look funny when you sleep, *amca*,' he said, 'your mouth blows in and out like a fish.'

'You're too old to get away with that sort of remark,' I said. 'You're just being rude.'

His shoulders heaved with laughter. 'And your legs,' he said, then slid round the door hastily as he saw me leap out of bed, 'I only came to tell you *baba* is home,' he said in an injured voice, 'and, anyway, it's true – you *did* look like a fish.'

I felt a good deal better after showering, and the faint wind from the sea was agreeable. Down in the harbour sails were silhouetted against the last blaze of the sun. In the slant of evening light outlines were blurred and softened and shadows lay in drifts of blue and purple in the folds of the distant hills. It was a peaceful scene.

I was touched to discover that for dinner a bottle of *rakı* had been put beside my place.

'I haven't tasted it for years,' I said to Mehmet. 'Will I get drunk, I wonder?'

Neighbours joined us for coffee. They questioned me about London and asked if I had ever been to America. They complained steadily and monotonously about the cost of living and envied Bedia the coffee I had brought as a present. Coffee, they said, was very difficult to get nowadays since the government had reduced imports, and in any case it was a terrible price.

The women were thirtyish, perhaps older. They dressed better than women of their class in London, but their faces were more lined. They all had painted fingernails and masses of chinking gold bracelets. Their husbands were doctors or engineers or army officers. Most of them belonged to the new professional class in Turkey. One of them, a staff captain with a command of three languages, was the son of a Kurdish tribesman; a middle-aged engineer was the son of an Ottoman general. They were charmingly provincial. They had mostly seen service in Ankara, were leaders of public opinion or society in their own *milieu* and rented summer villas for their holidays. Their children attended the same *lycées* and university, and the daughters married young. On Saturday nights they danced at the Officers' Club, celebrated the Cumhuriyet Bayram each year with fireworks, and disliked foreigners. They were literate but lacked polish. They all read at least one daily newspaper, the women liked looking at the American glossy magazines, and none of them cared what went on in the rest of the world. They spoke with amused contempt of the rich peasants who had invaded the city, occupying all the best houses. Their manner implied they were sophisticates marooned among barbarians.

Before turning in to sleep, Mehmet and I went for a walk along the front. From the opposite shore the lights reflected in the harbour water like beads on a string. A little coolness had come with night, but not enough to summon sleep. The heat of the vanished sun still oozed up from cobblestones and out of the walls of houses that had borne its weight all day. The burning stars looked enormous, and very near.

The cafés were open all night long. They were filled with bright-eyed, restless people in light suits who chattered and shouted to each other with the vivacity of daylight, and who all seemed to be eating ice-cream. We turned into a waterfront casino, whose lights sent out a pathway of gilt to the black water beyond. A tinny radio played national music against a background of talk. The music, in a distracted minor key, was tormenting, ruined by the terrible radio. We sipped iced coffee and talked, Mehmet diffident, anxious not to attract attention.

He was rectitude itself, and only mildly curious about my proposed wanderings. He was very dapper and gentlemanly, adjectives which would have pleased him, for he saw nothing derogatory in acting the part of the man of good breeding. He had changed little since schooldays, either in manner or appearance, and although he was far too polite to say so, I knew that he felt rather sorry for me. A brother who earned his living by writing was too precarious an asset to talk about; on seeing me, his air of surprise at my well-being was genuine, for he had no doubt expected to find me abjectly poor. He would have liked to see me in some settled occupation and had always regretted my decision to resign my commission as a regular officer in the Turkish Air Force. A writer in the family was rather hard luck, really, for they could never be sure what disgrace I would bring upon them. Furthermore, he was sceptical as to whether writing could ever make one rich.

'But I don't want to be rich,' I said. 'I want to be free.'

His only answer was a look of infinite pity.

An old friend of mine, recognising me from afar, shouted my name over the heads of the crowd. We beckoned him to join us and he threaded his way through the defeated-looking waiters and a group of men who were calling for a *tric-trac* set and sat down at our table.

'Well, by God,' he said, 'you're the last person I'd have expected to see here! I thought you'd have joined Nazım Hikmet in Moscow long ago.'

Nazım Hikmet is a brilliant Turkish poet who spent over ten years in

Turkish prisons during the Halk Partisi regime. He was released soon after the Menderes party came to power, and promptly escaped to Moscow where his too acute wit has since got him into trouble.

Mehmet, conscious of his position as a respectable member of democratic society, blenched and looked around him to see if there was anyone listening.

Our companion's name was Osman. He was a disreputable looking, devil-may-care journalist on an Izmir paper which was in constant trouble with the authorities and had been closed down at least once. It was a harmless foible with him to pretend that every writer was a Communist, or at least a fellow traveller. He was a man of fire, quoted passages from Shakespeare (in Turkish) for the confoundment of lesser mortals and had an unrelenting hatred for the Americans.

I had known him for a number of years. In his youth he had spent a good deal of time writing up the harrowing life stories of prostitutes in the Izmir bars. This lucrative period of his career had come to an end, however, when one of the prostitutes, objecting to being called 'a poor, misguided woman, dragged through the depths by man's degrading passions', attacked him with a breadknife and mutilated his face. The scars were still there. They pulled the left side of his face into a permanent leer and were the cause of his wife's throwing him over for another man.

He was as embittered as ever, insulting the government and the Americans at every opportunity. It was surely only a matter of time before he was clapped into prison for good. I could see that Mehmet was becoming restive, and to tell the truth I wasn't very comfortable either. Osman's violence was increasingly embarrassing. It seemed that at any moment he might start throwing glasses.

As we were leaving he said to me: 'If you're really going into Anatolia, you'd better leave that suit and that gold watch behind you or, by God, you'll not be a day's journey from Izmir before you find yourself without a stitch on you! Our peasants are no respecters of human life.'

The streets were still thronged with people. Water lapped gently against the harbour wall. A nearly full moon rode high, brilliant and remote. It was so bright that gardens were silvered, trees showed up bronze-green and on the nearer hills details of woods and crags stood out clearly. A few fishing-boats returning to shore were silhouetted in the silver path the moon threw over the sea. Kadife Kale lifted itself into the night, sombre as a pall. I could have walked all night.

During the day Mehmet was at the hospital, and I went out alone, eating lunch in little restaurants along the waterfront. I ran into Osman a few times, more by accident than design, although when he was sober he was a merry enough companion. He would have been a misfit in any society, chafing against restraint violently. He was so angry and bitter! He despised the masses because they had no learning and, unlike Mehmet, would have preferred to see me in rags.

'You can't earn money by telling the truth,' he said to me once, and almost in the same breath asked me how much I had paid for my shirt.

For the most part I went everywhere alone; sometimes, however, I was accompanied by the Afghan hound, who had made up his mind to put up with me, if not to love me.

Izmir by day is dull and nondescript. Only in the little side streets is there a breath of a more romantic past. Here, there is perpetual twilight in the cool sheltered houses with their closely grilled windows and deep stone arches. The streets are still cobbled, with weeds growing up between the stones. Lemon trees bloom in every garden.

The Izmir of the Ionian period was destroyed by the King of Sardis in 600BC, but Alexander the Great, inspired in a dream by the goddess Nemesis, built a new city on the slopes of Kadife Kale. Successively it was occupied by the Greeks and the Romans who crowned it with gymnasia, markets, theatres, houses, fountains and monuments. But little of the classical glory remains – part of the Golden Road only and the Sacred Way, traces of the *agora* on the hillside, sculptures of Poseidon and Demeter, and a network of underground shops. In the middle of an old burying ground is the mausoleum of Tantalus, whom Jupiter condemned to the torture of constant thirst while putting him within sight and sound of running water.

It has been a city since ancient times and recent excavations by Turkish archaeologists show evidence of a civilisation dating back to 2000BC. In fact, some of the urns unearthed are said to resemble Hittite urns dug up in central Anatolia, thus supposing cultural exchanges.

My most potent memory of Izmir had nothing to do with its changed appearance or with its new generation of stolid citizens. I had been that morning to the great new Kültür Park, where I paused for a time beside the figure of a bearded Roman god, whose marble hair is wreathed with flowers, and in whose arms is a cornucopia filled with the fruits of the Aegean region. Perhaps my head was filled with thoughts of classical Izmir, perhaps I was in a receptive enough mood to see gods walking in the streets. At any rate, I certainly caught sight of a young god in a garden. He was kneeling on the grass when I saw him, staring up at an old woman who seemed to be scolding him. It was a garden surrounded by trees, holding in its heart an old stone house with hooded, secret windows. It was a garden where anything might happen. At any moment the pipes of Pan himself might pierce the air. I halted beside the tall grilled gate, staring at the boy and the old woman, captivated by that smooth old-young olive face. What sensuality it expressed, what rapaciousness! He couldn't have been Turkish, for no Turkish face was ever carved with such delicacy, or such weakness. His beauty was in his weakness. He was Antinous, thwarted by the old woman of some trivial desire. He was Beauty and Evil. He was the Youth of Smyrna.

Like a figure on some Etruscan vase, he knelt there in the warm grass, his frozen gaiety, his quiescent passion, epitomising a grander era than this.

2

*The 'Fish Porters' – Ottoman Manisa – Travelling
Companions – Afyon – Konya – The Dumb Hotelier –
The First Yürük – Dervishes – Hikmet Bey – Meram*

I HAD INTENDED to spend some weeks in Izmir but by the end of the first week I was bored and longing for movement.

I had renewed acquaintance with one or two friends, and was amused to discover that certain Air Force customs had become hallowed by time. Take the case of the 'fish porters' for instance, the name we had given years ago to the unfortunate pilots who ferried fish between Izmir and Ankara for the delectation of a minister's palate.

The Aegean Sea is noted for the quality of its fish. When I was a junior officer, it was always suspected that to get on in life one only needed to be a general, for obvious reasons stationed in Ankara. To attract the attention of authority, nothing more strenuous was necessary than to lift the telephone, establish communication with the commanding officer of Izmir, and demand a dish of fish for the mighty. The amount of hard work this caused for the junior officers was unbelievable. In my youth, when all of us were more loyal to Atatürk's preachings than he was himself, we considered the waste of public money criminal. Nowadays, consciences are shelved and officers only burn with indignation at being kept so long in Izmir when they could do far better for themselves in Ankara.

The procedure for fishing was, and still is, elaborate. The general in

Ankara, brooding on the quickest way of obtaining favour, had nothing more to do than make the telephone call. Electrified into activity, the commanding officer in Izmir relayed the order to his adjutant. The adjutant promptly passed it on to the major, who passed it on to the captain, who passed it on to the most junior officer of all . . . All this, however, was the merest beginning. The first real hurdle the junior officer had to cross was the transport officer, always a surly fellow, who never had a car to loan, let alone an aeroplane. The officer in charge of the aircraft factory had next to be approached. He was a surly fellow too, who never learned from experience that it was necessary to keep in stock a supply of tin-lined wooden boxes for packing the fish. He was always full of excuses. There was no wood to spare, no tin for lining, no nails even, and even if all of them were to be had, there was no soldier who could be spared to put them together and make a box.

The junior officer, already treated like a dog, had also to put up with the vituperation of the officer in charge of supplies. This gentleman never curried favour, disdained rank and regarded all junior officers as fishmongers. The garrison commander was next on the list, for it was he who would supply the seaplane. This was not only the most important part of the whole operation but the one often attended by the most abuse.

By the time everything was laid on nobody cared any more what happened. Soldiers would arrive by the score, dynamite, rowing-boats, motorboats were assembled at strategic points, and the Izmir commanding officer – beaming with pride – would strut up and down the shore, certain of early promotion.

With charges of dynamite shooting up clouds of spray everywhere, and motorboats in danger of overturning rowing-boats, it was a wonder any fish were ever caught at all. However, everything always ended happily. Six perfect fish were selected for the Ankara minister, and six more for the general who had first thought of the idea. Packed in ice they were rushed off to the seaplane. A few minutes later the amphibious plane would sweep over our heads, off to the aerodrome, where the surly transport officer, out of sheer spite, would waste everyone's time pretending there was no aeroplane available to take the fish to Ankara. Ah, happy days!

The train journey to Konya was enlivened by the persistent snoring of a man with adenoids. He sat beside me (I had a corner seat, so it might have been worse), and every now and then, when the snores rose to a thin crescendo that sent a shudder down the sleeper's frame, I nudged him sharply. This had little effect, however, reducing him to asthmatic silence for less than a moment before the painful snoring was resumed again.

The train was crowded, the morning was bright, and I was in the benevolent mood that sometimes afflicts travellers. I was glad to be on the move again. The outskirts of Izmir disappeared from view, the last lime tree – growing up through a wall it had split in two – flung its green spray high against the morning sky and in the distance the sea heaved palely.

The train gathered speed, the adenoidal man groaned in his sleep and I kicked his shin. There sat opposite me a family of husband, wife and their son, about ten years old. They looked stolid and respectable. They disapproved of the snoring young man but they disapproved of me still more, for every time I gave the snorer a violent dig in the ribs or a kick on the shins, the woman pulled in her mouth and the man clicked his teeth.

'Allah, allah, *allah!*' he said to me once. 'Leave him to sleep in peace!'

The sun poured in, roasting us. The man opposite took off his tie and his jacket and wiped his neck with a handkerchief. His wife fanned herself with a newspaper and kept up a low murmuring complaint. The child said he was thirsty. I winked at him and he put out his tongue, quickly and slyly, turning his head rapidly sideways to see if his mother had observed.

Entering Manisa the train slowed down. Manisa is one of the most typical of Ottoman cities and its skyline is dominated by the minarets of mosques. As Magnesia, it was a battlefield where the Romans defeated

Antiochus, driving him back beyond the Taurus Mountains. As Manisa, it was a favourite resort of early Ottoman sultans. Murat II, who first abdicated in 1444, came to live in Manisa, but returned to defeat the Hungarians at the Battle of Varna. He built a palace at Manisa, little trace of which remains, in whose gardens he spent a great deal of time meditating on the mysteries of life and death. The town is built on the slopes of Mount Manisa, and there are abundant orchards rising above the plain. There are some fine buildings there, mainly the mosques built by Murat III and the *medresse*, or sacred college, now turned into a museum of Ottoman art.

Leaving the station we picked up speed again. On both sides of us were vineyards where women and children were working with great diligence. Through the trees I saw lorries, horses and carts, even donkeys, and men wheeling wicker baskets.

The man opposite me said: 'It's a terrible disaster, isn't it?'

I did not apprehend his meaning at first, and merely nodded my head, but his wife said impatiently: 'Didn't you know that half the grape crop has been lost?'

I didn't know, although I had heard that the drought had been bad this year. My companions told me that the whole of Anatolia was suffering, and that the grapes had shrivelled on the vine. Harvesting, which usually took place in August, was a month ahead. The intensely cold winter, and the – even for Anatolia – unusually dry summer had taken their toll; owners of vineyards were already prophesying their own ruination. At every station we passed, tall baskets of grapes stood on the platform. Sometimes water melons, which had done well, were piled beside them awaiting transport to the cities. The feverish activity of the grape-pickers followed us right down the line.

My companions were resigned to loss. They spoke of earthquake and flood, of Ankara burning under the sun while Çankırı, a short distance away, froze with unseasonable cold.

'The cost of living will go up again,' said the woman, pathetically knowledgeable.

'But Menderes says there's no cost-of-living problem in the country,' I replied.

Her husband snorted angrily. 'If you ask him,' he said, 'everyone's stomach is full, but ask *me*, I'll tell you what I think!'

He proceeded to tell me – eloquently, hardly pausing for breath, his anger threatening to get the better of him all the time. He stopped when we reached Alaşehir, but that was only because he was getting off. Even from the platform he shouted back a few more bits of illuminating information.

'Ask me if I can buy coffee,' he shouted, but the train was already moving, so I never heard the rest of it.

We climbed the mountains towards Afyon and the air grew deliciously cooler. The country here was bleak and featureless, only occasionally relieved by glimpses of huge, distant forests. I had to change trains at Afyon, and as I pulled my suitcase from the luggage rack it hit my snoring companion a crack on the head. He awoke immediately, leaping up with clenched fists and a string of curses. He glared all round the carriage, then subsided into his seat once more. He was already asleep again before the train pulled to a stop. I left him snoring.

At Afyon an indifferent porter told me that the train for Konya, the Meram Express, was not leaving before evening. I left my case and walked into the town, a pleasant walk along acacia-lined roads. I was glad to stretch my legs after so many hours in the train.

The clear light of afternoon paled the tops of the mountains, and the cool aromatic air of the uplands was a delight after day-long heat. The walk was longer than I had anticipated, however, and I was glad when the great ironstone fortress loomed up in front of me – almost like some prehistoric monster. I had not met a soul on the way in, and I was conscious of hunger and the need for companionship. The stark clear lines of the hillsides were already turning to umber. The outcrops and jagged peaks of rocks, and the dark foliage gathered in the hollows, looked primeval and unbelievably savage.

The town was dusty, scented with acacia trees and the cool mountain air. Lights were already being turned on in some of the small shops. A mound of cheese filled the window of one, lengths of *pastırma* festooned another. The twin minarets of a mosque stuck up to heaven like the spars of a boat. The streets were narrow and cobbled, and I quenched my thirst at a fountain that was a gem of Ottoman art. I passed a coffee shop, where the smell tempted me in. It was full of civil-servant types, in tight striped trousers and wing collars. I felt I must have strayed into the past. They sat drinking coffee, relaxing after the day's work, all of them talking together, intent on airing their own views rather than listening to those of their neighbours. They stared as I walked in, momentarily silenced, weighing me up, their alert eyes speculating on my business among them. I ordered coffee, and conversation flowed back again. They talked of women and the high cost of living; the subjects were beginning to have a repetitive flavour.

One of the men detached himself from a group and came over to my table. He asked me, in French, if I would care to join his table. I replied in Turkish that I was quite happy where I was, but that if he cared to join me, I should be delighted. When he discovered I was a Turk, the patina of hospitality vanished from his face and he looked morose. He sat down, however, and I ordered coffee for him. He said he worked for the town council, that it was a dog's life and that he earned barely enough to keep himself alive. He had, moreover, a wife and three children to support, and an aged mother, who was a widow. One of his daughters would be marrying next year, God be thanked, but he didn't know where he'd get money to pay for the wedding celebrations. Presently a few more of his companions drifted over and I ordered more coffees. One of them had been trained as an engineer in America, and was proud to introduce Americanisms into the conversation. I asked him why he had returned to Turkey.

'To do my army service,' he said, shrugging his shoulders. 'If I hadn't come back they'd have taken away my Turkish nationality, and now I haven't the money to go anywhere else.'

They questioned me exhaustively, and after learning that I had lived in London for nearly ten years, grew denunciatory. Why did I not live in my own country? How did I earn money? Did the rest of the world think Turkey was doing well? Did they recognise her as a modern nation? I prevaricated. It was no use telling these earnest civil servants that the rest of the world didn't give a damn about Turkey, they wouldn't have believed me anyway. Their pride and their belief in themselves was enormous. One of them told me that he had bought a refrigerator for his wife, another boasted that soon he would be sending his son to Ankara University.

Since my train did not leave until half-past nine, the engineer invited me to his home for dinner. He was married to the only woman dentist in Afyon and they had a son of six. His wife was a pleasant product of new Turkey, a slim little woman who was a lively conversationalist and had few illusions about Turkey's position in the world. She had been born and bred in Afyon, educated at Istanbul University, and had had a further year's study in America. She liked living in Afyon, admired change, but regretted too much Westernisation.

'First, we must prove ourselves to ourselves,' she said, and showed off all her pearly teeth in a brilliant smile.

Her house was small and pleasant. There were Sparta carpets on the floors of hall and sitting-room, and cane furniture. We ate a superb dish of *imam bayaldı*, young aubergines cooked in olive oil and garlic, and she deplored the dreadful habit of eating from tins which had spread even as far as Afyon. Her mother, who lived with them, did all the cooking, but she herself had learned how to cook too.

'We shall soon have so few national characteristics left,' she said, 'that it is necessary at least to preserve our cooking.'

They were not rich, and lived very simply. They had no car, no servant and no refrigerator.

'What's wrong with the well in the garden?' my hostess asked, when her husband spoke of their neighbours, who seemed to have everything, and she took me out to the garden to show me the well. It reminded me of my childhood – that great round tower rising out of a concrete floor.

Ropes, with metal baskets suspended from them, were fastened securely to the sides of the concrete 'tower'. She hauled up one of the ropes to show me the basket of grapes, tomatoes and packaged butter which had been resting in the water. They were cold as ice. Peering down into the black depths I could see no trace of water, although I heard its gurgling as the basket was lowered once more.

'This is *my* refrigerator,' she said.

In the end I left it too late to walk back to the station and an obliging neighbour with a car had to drive me there. I rescued my bag and hurled myself on to the Meram Express just before it moved off. It was crowded, and I spent the entire night in the corridor beside the lavatory. Even the lavatory was occupied by a mother and two young children, who could be heard crying at intervals.

We reached Konya at five o'clock the next morning, an impossible hour to arrive anywhere. I felt sleepy and dirty, and hoped I hadn't acquired any lice from my tightly packed companions of the night. There was no taxi to be had but a porter directed me to a hotel, which he said was only a stone's throw away. Perhaps he had a long arm, or perhaps I was too sleepy to notice it. At any rate I didn't find it.

The morning was cool, pleasantly crisp, but the hills were veiled in mist, forerunner of heat later in the day. The main boulevard, shuttered, patently still asleep, was long, tree-lined, and of identical pattern with a thousand boulevards all over the country. A cat lay sleeping outside a baker's shop and as I stooped to tickle its ears the door of the shop opened and an enormous man in his nightshirt started to take down the shutters. I asked where I would find a hotel, and in a thick, morning voice, he gestured down a side-street. But one side-street led to another and after a while I grew used to the idea of touring Konya on foot. I came out on a big green square, where there was a charming mosque set in a garden, and found a hotel close by. It was closed, of course. What else had I expected?

I banged on the door, and after several minutes it was opened by a man in a striped nightshirt and a *kaftan* wound about his head. He motioned to me to enter, hiding a yawn with a hairy hand, and I followed him up a flight of precipitous stairs. They creaked loudly under our feet, and once I stumbled and the man in the nightshirt, some way ahead of me, turned threateningly. At least, I took it to be a threatening gesture. He only needed a scimitar to complete the picture of a fierce Ottoman warrior about to slaughter the infidel. At last we emerged on to a small landing. He showed me into a room with two beds, gestured to the one beside the window and then left me. He hadn't spoken a word.

I was tired. I took off my jacket and shoes, patted the revolver that travelled everywhere with me, and lay down on the bed that was to be mine. The other one had not been slept in, and I debated whether I should offer to pay for the whole room now or wait until my privacy was threatened. I must have slept, for the next thing I remember was waking to a slight noise beside me. I sat up, feeling for my revolver and my watch. The man who had opened the door to me, now dressed in a pair of baggy trousers and an open-necked shirt, had just put a bowl of warm water and a clean towel on the table beside the bed. I ordered a glass of lemon tea. He nodded and went out. I made up my mind he was dumb.

After shaving and dressing I went out in search of a man I had met in London who lived in or near Konya. His name was Hikmet Bey, and when I met him he had been one of a group of Turkish landowners touring English farms, studying farming conditions. I had forgotten his surname and his address, retaining nothing but the memory of a bull-like man who had invited me to visit him if ever I reached Konya.

It was a hot, breezy day. The wind blew the dust of the roads into eddies, covering trees and gardens with a thin grey film. Against a background of deep blue, fluffy white clouds scudded before the wind.

Konya was clean and smug, newly washed by a shower of rain that must have fallen while I slept. Here and there gay pink houses stood out in sharp contrast among the more uniform greys and dirty creams. The public gardens, as integral a part of modern Turkish life as the broad white boulevards, were ablaze with scarlet geraniums. At a first glance there seemed to be few remains of Selcuk architecture, which in Konya reached its apex. Even the public gardens are built on the mound of the old citadel.

The city, known to the Romans as Iconium, is built high above sea level. The air is bracing. Wherever one looks, there are blue mountains rising on the horizon like islands from the sea. Only to the north does the flat plain vanish in brown distance. The city lies in a burst of green, due to the streams gushing from the mountains of Pisidia.

It is a prosperous place where sheep and grain farming are the main money spinners. Side by side with new shops, all glass and chromium, are the ruined Selcuk buildings, dating from the eleventh century. Here and there old wooden houses, two-storeyed, the upper part projecting over the street, are flanked by squat new houses, extravagantly white. Behind the main boulevard lie street after street of open markets, where traders make and sell their goods. Many of the streets are still cobbled and the *araba*, drawn by two high-stepping horses, is still the most popular form of transport. Peasants from neighbouring villages use the *yaylı*, the high sides painted in vivid colours, the harness of the horses gay with ribbons, and blue beads to ward off the Evil Eye. Not so very many years ago, the *yaylı* was used to deliver mail in villages and towns outside Konya. The minarets of mosques are everywhere.

Near the market section is a wide square from where the camel caravans set off on their long trek across the plain. It was here that I saw the first nomad, a Yürük from the mountains above the city. He stood there with his camel, already laden for the homeward journey, wearing a shaggy goatskin coat, his baggy trousers tucked into the tops of long boots. His face was the colour of leather, his nose as hooked as some carving on a Hittite bas-relief. He swung himself on to the camel, a small boy with a heavily laden donkey hurrying after him, and loped towards the plain, the swaying and heaving of the camel, with its erect small head, churning my stomach in time with its motion.

According to Greek legend, Perseus, the son of Jupiter and Danae, came to Konya to slay the Gorgon. Having cut off her head, he hung it on a pillar, and thus gave the name of Iconium to the city – meaning 'the place of the image'. Another legend asserts it was the first city to emerge from the Deluge, in which all men had perished. Prometheus, instructed by Jupiter, made images or 'icons' of mud, which came to life when the wind blew on them, thus repopulating Iconium.

It came under the domination of the Hittites, Phrygians, Lydians, Graeco-Persians and Romans. During Roman times it became one of the earliest centres of Christianity. In 1097, it was made the capital of the Selcuk Empire, and rose to the peak of its splendour as a Selcuk city in the early thirteenth century. It is still richly endowed with Selcuk monuments. In 1466 it became part of the Ottoman Empire.

The mosque of Alaaddin, named after the Selcuk sultan, is situated on a hill and is excellently preserved. It was completed in the year 1221 and is one of the oldest Turkish mosques. It is built of a soft red-gold stone and is vast in size, although very plain compared with the later ornamental mosques of the Ottomans. Grouped around it are the impressive tombs of Alaaddin and his family, enclosed by a high-niched octagonal wall richly decorated with faience tiles. The *medresse* is part of the group and is famous for the black and light-blue tiles which cover the walls and dome.

The Ince Minaret was built in 1265 as a university by a Selcuk vizier. Its gate is a triumph of Selcuk art, as are the remains of the minaret, the upper half of which was struck by lightning within the last century. The surviving half is delicately built, faced with turquoise blue tiles that seem to shimmer with translucency in early evening light.

Konya too was the home of the Mevlevi Dervishes. Celaleddin, of Persian origin, founded the Order of Dervishes on pantheistic doctrines, giving them poetic expression. The religion was calm, philosophic and mystical, seeking union with the Infinite in trancelike dancing – a sort of whirling really, like that of a spinning top, the long pleated skirts of the Mevlevi flaring out from the dancer's waist like a ballerina's skirt. The Dervishes flourished in Ottoman Turkey and deviated from Orthodox Islam in their policy of non-violence and the tacit implication that the Dervish found God in his own way.

Their home is now a museum, a place of calm exaltation where their spirit still lingers. Deep purple shadows seem to people dark corners with wraiths of long ago; an eddy of dust might be Celaleddin himself rising from the past, hands above his head, the left palm facing earthward, the right straining to heaven, symbolising the urgent desire to fly to the Divine Spirit that activated him. The museum is crowded with relics. There are handwritten Korans, one of which dates back a thousand years. There are exquisite rugs of seven hundred years ago.

The paved courtyard itself is an invitation to step back to the calm past of the Dervishes. Flowering cherry blooms through the spring, tall poplars shade it in summer, and all year long the pigeons – dove grey, ochre-rose and pearly white – keep up their persistent cooing. There is a fountain, exquisitely carved. With sunlight slanting greenly through the trees, it seems to give off an aura of eternal peace.

Dominating the courtyard are the tombs of holy men. Celaleddin and his father are there. Each tomb is a work of art in its own right – carved, tiled and gilded with signs from the Koran. Through the high, fretted windows the sun pours in solemn splendour. The rich hangings of silk and velvet glow like jewels. Celaleddin's tomb is covered with a green velvet pall, lavishly embroidered in faded gold. The flutes and the reeds, to which the Dervishes danced, hang useless on the walls above the tombs. The enormous turbans and the cone-shaped hats have become glass-case exhibits, curiosities for the modern Turkish child to regard with indifference.

The order of Dervishes was gay and hospitable. They loved music and dancing. They drank wine, which they offered to the stranger. Charity and benevolence were the essence of their teaching. They were abolished in 1925 by Kemal Atatürk, who declared them reactionary and a source of danger to his Republic.

I lunched in a dim restaurant off the main boulevard, where a collarless waiter served excellently cooked *pirzola* and talked incessantly of Istanbul where he longed to go. Courteously he turned on the radio for me, so that I might listen to the news from Ankara. Gramophone records followed the news and the waiter – neglecting to bring me the next course – beat his hands softly in time with the music and looked pleased when I admired his pleasant tenor voice.

After lunch, I wandered back to the market again and watched an American buying a pottery water-gourd for which he paid far too much. Peasants, in for a day's shopping, were to be seen everywhere. So were the wild horsemen of the plains and a party of colourfully dressed Yürük, who bartered rush baskets for a sack of flour.

I had been carried away by what I had seen, and had still not found anyone who knew Hikmet Bey. However, in the market, I found a group of old men outside a coffee shop who recognised his name at once. By the tone of their voices when they mentioned him, it was obvious that he was rich and well respected. They fingered their amber beads and talked in cracked old voices, exquisitely courteous. They asked me where I came from and I replied Istanbul, feeling that London was too far away to convey anything to them.

I ordered a round of coffees and they dipped their lumps of sugar, sucking them noisily, and spoke of Hikmet Bey. They had seen him not an hour ago. They called the boy who was serving coffee.

'Go, run and find Hikmet Bey Efendi for this gentleman from Istanbul. He will be in the market somewhere. Run, now, quickly!'

The owner of the shop appeared, divesting the boy of the brass tray that hung round his neck with chains, and I apologised for causing so much trouble.

'Efendi, *beyim*, nothing is too much trouble. You are our guest. You have come a long way to find Hikmet Bey Efendi, who as all Konya knows is our greatest man!'

I thought it charming that he should express himself so courteously, and in return pretended not to notice when he grossly overcharged me for the coffees. After all, one cannot have everything in this life.

Hikmet Bey was located successfully and came back with the boy.

He wrung my hand until I thought it would drop off and kissed my cheeks many times, after each salutation stepping back to survey me anew.

'What happy wind blew you as far as Konya?' he boomed.

He was tall, with immensely powerful shoulders and a great laugh that seemed to rumble right up from his belly. He was overcome with the emotion of seeing me, and by the time he stopped slapping my back and kissing me and pumping my hand up and down, I felt sure I should have bruises the size of eggs. He bubbled over with good humour and energy. He cracked jokes with the old men, tweaked the boy's ear lingeringly, afterwards raising ecstatic eyes to heaven, and had the coffee shop owner holding his sides with laughter. He was all dash and verve, yet as solid and dependable as a rock. His laughter was gargantuan and infectious. While we talked, I looked at him affectionately. I remembered a story I had once heard of him.

He had been an officer stationed on the Russian–Turkish border for two years, without relief and without leave. Hikmet was thirty at the time, with enough virility for two men. For two years he hadn't seen a woman, not even a peasant woman, and according to the officer telling me the story, there wasn't even a donkey that the soldiers hadn't requisitioned for themselves. Poor Hikmet suffered, but not in silence. Week by week, passionate letters were dispatched by him to Ankara. These were ignored. He might have been left on the border for ever, had he not conceived the happy idea of writing to Kemal Atatürk himself. His letter was ignored, however, probably destroyed by a superior young lieutenant. Hikmet allowed several weeks to pass, and then – by means of a soldier who had finished his national service and was returning to his own town – despatched the following telegram to Atatürk:

ARE YOU ALIVE OR ARE YOU DEAD. IF YOU ARE ALIVE WHY DON'T YOU ANSWER MY LETTERS. IF YOU ARE DEAD THEN I MIGHT AS WELL BE.

The telegram duly reached Atatürk, who made enquiries, and gave orders for Hikmet to be transferred elsewhere.

Hikmet, summoned to Istanbul, stepped off the train in the full glory of his uniform and headed straight away for the first brothel. One of the deadliest sins for a Turkish officer is to go to a brothel in uniform. Hikmet, past caring, intoxicated as a wild ram after so much abstinence, spent the day in the brothel, and was arrested towards midnight, when some of his brothers-in-arms, decently disguised as civilians, reported him to the military police.

Questioned at military police headquarters by an officer several years his junior, Hikmet lost his temper and set about smashing the furniture. He was taken to the commanding officer, who turned out to be a reasonable colonel. He listened to both sides of the story carefully. At the end he said: 'Well, lieutenant, thank God he went to the brothel first, otherwise you or I would be in danger from him. I think you'd better let him go back and spend the night where you found him. Lend him a coat and a pair of trousers.'

We finished our third round of coffee, and Hikmet said we would go back to the hotel and collect my bag. He insisted I should be his guest as long as I remained in Konya. Unfortunately, I had forgotten the name of my hotel and we spent fruitless time going in and out of small, shabby places that all looked exactly like the hotel I had entered that morning. We found it at last, my case was recovered, and we whirled out of Konya's dust in Hikmet Bey's big American car.

The road to Meram, where he lived, was indifferent, but the scenery was splendid. The fields were golden with corn and the paler tint of wheat and flocks of sheep grazed on the plain. Groups of poplars threw velvety shadows on the road before us, and once we crossed a rickety bridge supported by five stone arches. Beside a stream we saw a king-fisher, vividly beautiful in his blue overcoat and russet breast. Farther along the same road we came across a stork, contemplating life on one leg. He flew away before we reached him, his long legs dangling, and his body dazzlingly white in the sun. We met few people on the road. Once we passed a tribesman from beyond the Taurus on a rangy horse as wild looking as himself, which shied even before the car came abreast of him at all. A caravan of camels loped by in the opposite direction and we stopped the car for them to pass. The leading camel was an obstinate fellow who refused to budge until his owner jumped down to pull him forcibly by his rope. He shuddered as he was manoeuvred past the car, groaned, and pulled back his rubbery lips from his teeth in a savage snarl.

We turned in at a pair of broken-down gates and were at once surrounded by a pack of dogs, who milled about the car, barking, leaping and generally going into an ecstasy of love for Hikmet Bey.

3

'Dogs bark . . . ' – Peasant Problems – Snakes – A Model Farm – Village Institutes – Catching our Dinner – Erotic Dancing

HIKMET got out of the car, leaving me cowering in my seat. He talked soothingly to the saliva-dripping dogs, with their sharp-spiked collars, worn as a safeguard against the wolves, then he called to me to join him.

'Are you sure I won't be torn limb from limb?' I asked, making no attempt to move and pleased with the protection – however flimsy – of thick glass windows between me and the dogs.

'Come along, come along,' said Hikmet Bey impatiently. 'You've got to face them sometime, for God's sake.'

Emerging gingerly, I remained beside the door of the car, the dogs growling softly in their throats. Hikmet Bey made a great to-do of introducing me to each dog – who all had fearsome names like Black Wolf, Ferocious Tiger and so on. I had reached the stage of idiotic fright where I wondered if it would be in order to bow to each dog in turn, acknowledging the introduction. Hikmet Bey, solemn as an owl, explained to the dogs that I was a friend and must be treated as a friend. One or two of them barked sharply, perhaps signifying their disapproval – or maybe even their approval, for after he had talked to them they snuffled round me, wagged their tails, and one of them even ventured to lick my hand. I shuddered, not daring to trust them an inch. However, as soon as they realised I was not going to attack Hikmet Bey, they became indifferent and wandered away on their own business.

'They are good faithful creatures,' said Hikmet Bey fondly, 'and one must never insult their intelligence. We always make a point of introducing them to guests and then they know everything is all right.'

I followed him up to the house, along a well-gravelled path. Vineyards spread away on either side, as well as fig orchards. Hikmet Bey complained of the poor year he had had. Nearly a quarter of his men were away on National Service and the grapes had withered on the vine.

When we came in sight of the long veranda behind the house, I was surprised to see many people sitting there. It was unreasonable to be surprised, yet I realised I had never known anything about Hikmet Bey, perhaps supposing him to be a solitary. That he might have a wife, children, other relatives, was as much of a shock to me as was our sudden appearance to the people on the veranda. There were little feminine shrieks of dismay, and three of the women disappeared into the house without waiting for us. The remaining woman drew a silk scarf across her head, covering part of her face.

'*Eşekler!* [donkeys],' Hikmet Bey exploded. 'Anyone would think they'd never seen a man in their lives! Do you know they're running away to cover up their faces because you're a stranger? Come back,' he yelled after the retreating women. 'We're not going to eat you!'

There was a dignified silence from the veranda, even the men refusing to smile at Hikmet Bey's sally.

Hikmet Bey sighed. 'Dogs bark but the caravan moves on,' he quoted. 'Even after thirty-three years of a republic they won't change their ways. There's no use talking to them, they go on behaving as their mothers did before them.'

We climbed the six broken steps up to the veranda, the men coming forward to greet us but the seated woman barely touching the tips of our fingers in acknowledgement. The other women were induced by Hikmet Bey's bellowing to come out of the house. They now wore embroidered headscarves, which every now and then they remembered to draw up over their chins, successfully hiding them-selves from male eyes.

A young girl of about eleven served us with coffee and glasses of spring water. She was a beautiful child with the flowing black curls and speaking eyes of the mountain Turk. She did not appear to be a relative.

I was given the best chair, while Hikmet Bey flung himself down on the tiles beside me. He said jocularly to his son: 'Irfan Bey comes from London, Nuri' – he gestured to the boy to come nearer – 'so he knows how English should be spoken. Let us hear you speaking English with him, so that I may know whether the thousands of lira you're costing me each year at the *lycée* in Istanbul are being well spent or are merely providing an excuse for you to buy tea and cakes for your girlfriends in the Hilton Hotel.'

Nuri threw me a look of purest hate.

'Well?' asked his father. 'Have you lost your tongue?'

'I am so glad you haf come,' said Nuri.

His father turned to look up at me. 'Did he speak English?' he asked me.

'Yes, indeed,' I said. 'He said he was glad I was here.'

'Good. He must speak some English with you every day.'

Nuri drifted away to a corner, but I could see that he was smouldering, and every now and then he would glance across at me unhappily. My presence would probably ruin the rest of his holidays.

People kept coming and going, and I soon lost track of them. In fact it took me several days before I was able to establish their kinship with Hikmet Bey. That first afternoon there were, I think, fifteen people on the veranda at times. Of these, I remember his wife, his five children, a brother-in-law, his brother-in-law's wife and two children, and a nephew from Diyarbekır who was recuperating after an illness. The others were no more than flitting shadows, vague shapes that mumbled greetings or pushed a glass of grape juice into one's hands.

The women were uncomfortable in my presence, but the terror inspired by Hikmet Bey's commanding demeanour kept them rooted to their seats. They never spoke unless they were asked a direct question, and then they would reply in whispers, with eyes downcast and their hands folded sedately in their laps. I never heard one of them express an opinion or put herself forward in any way. The dogs had indeed barked, and continued to bark, but the women were impervious. Like the caravan they went on their way regardless.

Hikmet Bey's father, who came to stay while I was there, was an almost comic character. He seemed to spend most of his time running after the beautiful eleven-year-old child, or making obscene shadow play with his fingers on sunlit walls. He liked quoting old proverbs, which seemed the sole extent of his knowledge. Over a cup of coffee he would say sententiously: 'A cup of coffee commits one to forty years of friendship.' The first evening he was with us, he said, apropos of nothing at all but looking meaningfully at me: 'A guest comes with ten blessings. He eats one and leaves nine.' On the question of chastisement for Nuri, who had deeply offended Hikmet Bey on some matter, he said: 'A tree should be bent when young.' The greatest doubts entered my mind, however, when he said slyly and looking at me in the most unmistakable fashion: 'A wise man remembers his friends at all times, a fool only when he is in need of them.' Altogether he had a very poor opinion of me, and when told that I was a writer, asked if it wasn't better to shoot myself. Hikmet Bey, who had not harvested his grapes with enough speed while there were any to harvest, was told: 'Big head, big headache.' The old man never had to do anything more than quote his proverbs; their few words expressed his feelings trenchantly. The whole family treated him with great respect and nobody ever put a stop to his unmerciful chasing of the Kurdish child. By night, when all the rest of the household were sleeping, I would hear him padding about on the landing, up to God knows what nefarious work.

My room overlooked the gardens, a tangle of weeds and wild grasses but with a view of distant wheatfields. Sleep was difficult, however, what with the lecherous old man pottering about on the landing and the deep-throated growls of the dogs every so often. Sometimes a flock of wild geese would pass by overhead, the silver threads of their cries sounding sharply in the quiet night. In the marshes near the house, frogs croaked all through the night, an interminable swelling murmur that when it died away left one listening for it to start again.

There was little to do, except relax. Time was my own, but because the whole area seemed to be snake infested, I was driven to sitting on the veranda, which meant that the women stayed in the house, or accompanying Hikmet Bey to Konya where he had a great deal of business. There were always visitors, but not always to pay social visits. Hikmet Bey being a man of substance, and an educated man at that, was often called on to settle local disputes. The peasants had a dislike of going to law and avoided the Konya police like the plague.

The curious phraseology of government or legal documents is as much of a nightmare in Turkey as anywhere else in the world, and although the peasants about Meram were literate, they never trusted themselves to decipher the forms that from time to time descended on them like a shower from heaven. Forms telling them about crop requirements, hygiene against pests or local health regulations flummoxed them, and they would appear on Hikmet Bey's veranda, waving their little pieces of paper, meekly apologetic.

Hikmet Bey's nephew, Dursun, sometimes deputised for his uncle. Sometimes I was called on to give the benefit of my advice but generally I couldn't make head or tail of the forms either. So many things had changed since I had left Turkey – not least the language. I often found myself straining to decipher what Nuri, representative of the younger generation, was saying, and it seemed to me that there was, indeed there is, a tendency towards a new stylisation of language, a formality that, although a mere feeble ghost in comparison with the ornate language of the Ottomans, used words less for their precise meanings than as ornamentation. It is true the tendency must be regarded as slight, and whether it is anything more than a fashion among the intellectuals and the literate younger generation remains to be seen.

One morning, an old peasant called, as usual waving a piece of printed paper in his hands. Hikmet Bey was in Konya so, after greeting us, the peasant said to Dursun Bey: 'I can't understand this *gavur* [infidel] language at all. I have six grandchildren, and they don't understand what I say and I can't understand what they say either. It's all this teaching. We used to say, "He went to the garden," but they say, "Went to the garden he," with a whole lot of other words I can't make out at all mixed up with what they're telling me.' He shook his head, proffering the bit of paper to Dursun Bey to translate. 'It's not Turkish they speak any more,' he said.

Dursun Bey told the old man that the bit of paper was a notification of a summons to court. Hearing this, our visitor became excited.

'The son of a donkey!' he shouted. 'That Hasan, that son and grandson of a prostitute! May the worms gnaw his vitals!'

Hasan, apparently, had reported the old man to the police for assaulting him when he refused to pay the price of two sheep that had been killed by Hasan's borrowed tractor.

Another day, a man came with a complaint about his prospective son-in-law. Hikmet Bey happened to be at home, so Dursun Bey and I were relieved of the necessity of making a decision.

Our visitor was about fifty, a fine upstanding man with hirsute hands and wrists and a tattered shirt open to his navel. He told us that his daughter was betrothed to a young man who, taking advantage of her innocence, had seduced her in his father's barn. He now refused to marry her, saying she was no longer a virgin, and refused also to return the two cows that had been presented to him as part of her dowry. Furthermore, in order to avoid arrest himself on a charge of rape, he said it was not he who had seduced the girl. His father and brothers swore they had seen a man, a stranger to them, leaving the barn with the girl.

Hikmet Bey, chin on hands, listened attentively, nodding his head now and then when his visitor made a point he agreed with. At the end he advised the man to report the matter to the police in Konya. The man replied he'd rather die than become involved with the police. Hikmet

Bey shrugged and said that if his daughter was telling the truth it was a matter for the police. The man went away dissatisfied and Hikmet Bey said to us: 'He won't go to the police because he thinks it will bring disgrace on the family. You'll see, he'll settle matters himself. There'll be an accident, someone will be killed. It always ends that way.'

But this time it did not, for before I left Konya I heard that the girl's father had beaten up the young man, who was now taking him to court. In the meantime every peasant in the district had heard the story and put their own construction on it.

However, there were days when nobody called at all, and on such days I found it very pleasant to relax on the veranda, sometimes alone, sometimes with Dursun Bey. I never tired of watching the bright darting birds swooping down for the crumbs I always carried for them. After a time pigeons began driving them out. In Turkey, pigeons are grossly overfed and are never killed since Turks regard them as the little messengers of God – a relic of the Noah's Ark story.

There were so many birds and at first I could recognise only the more obvious – the song-thrush, the blackbird, the house-martin. But soon, with the aid of binoculars and the knowledgeable Nuri beside me, I discovered the birds which were too wild and shy to descend to the veranda for crumbs. In the apple-orchard we found goldfinches, crimson and white and brilliant yellow, with liquid voices that melted the heart. Once we discovered a blue tit creeping up a tree-trunk to hang head downwards from a thick branch. Tiring of this game, he righted himself to look around, surprised and black eyed, and began to scold some invisible companion. Presently another blue tit flew out of the tree and the pair flew away together. Their colouring was intense, especially the yellow belly and the clear-blue tufted crown. The green woodpecker was another favourite of mine, and the pair we saw in Hikmet Bey's orchard spent their time running up and down trees then shouting 'ha-ha' at each other, their fiery crowns and moustaches quivering.

There was a family of redstarts, who flew about busily, catching insects in the air, their bright crimson tails trembling in a sort of ecstasy.

Once I made a too rapid movement and one of them sent out the alarm to the others – a sharp metallic call that sent the whole family sailing away over my head, a vivid and unforgettable streak of colour against a hot blue sky.

Country life was instructive – a delightful existence, had it not been for the snakes that slithered unexpectedly across one's path when we were out walking or uncoiled themselves from harmless-looking trees. While I was in Hikmet Bey's house I heard the awful story of the young peasant woman who, falling asleep in the fields, had swallowed a snake. She was saved by the presence of mind of her mother who lit a fire of brushwood, boiled some milk and held the girl's head over it. The snake, fascinated by the smell of the milk, emerged from her throat and was battered to death with a large stone. I have always been terrified of snakes and for a week after I heard this story I dreamt of snakes every night, and during the day was afraid to fall asleep on the veranda.

However, apart from the snakes, my idyllic existence was also marred by the lavatories. One of these was downstairs, just inside the hall door. Windowless and full of abominable odours, its presence pervaded the whole house. Some sort of water system had been rigged up, but the pressure was insufficient. The water flowed lethargically from a tap placed too high on the wall, splashing the tiles and one's feet alike. It wound its way slowly to the too-shallow channel, arriving as little more than a trickle at the site of operations. It was the sort of place to avoid at all costs. But it had had its uses. Hikmet Bey told me that when he was a small boy an aunt by marriage used to excuse herself from her husband's presence and receive her lover through the window of the lavatory. The husband, discovering this, had the window taken away and the space bricked up. He subsequently divorced his faithless wife who thereupon entered a high-class brothel in Istanbul.

The other lavatory was a contrived affair in the garden, a perilous journey away at any time, since rats lurked in the vicinity, but a positively fearsome experience at night when the light of a torch might reveal a pair of shining eyes – rat or snake? One never dared investigate.

Dursun Bey and I soon became good friends and I promised that if ever I got as far as Diyarbekır I would visit him. He was a broker, buying figs and sultanas from Izmir and rice from Bursa. He was a large man, very sensitive to his bulk, a slow thinker, level-headed and completely honest. His greatest enjoyment was to spend a day fishing, returning in the evening with a basket of trout or carp, which he insisted on having cooked for dinner. There was one period when we were eating fish twice a day, for Dursun Bey seemed to be having unusual luck and Hikmet Bey was too mean to throw the fish away. As he said to me: 'What can one do? There's all this fish here, someone's got to eat it. After all, it's an insult to God to throw it away.'

We discovered, through Nuri, that Dursun Bey's luck was not quite what we had thought. In an effort to impress, and tired of Hikmet Bey's jibes that he spent his days catching nothing, he had made a bargain with two or three peasants who sold their fish to him.

Hikmet Bey drove us out to Kavakli to see his farm. It was so isolated that we might have been in the middle of nowhere. The farm was fully mechanised and was the pride and joy of Hikmet Bey's heart. He boasted proudly that nowhere in England or Germany had he seen such a well-equipped farm. I was ready to believe him so far as concerned a quantity of shining tractors, and silos to house grain, and all the other complicated machinery that is turning the land into a vast open-air factory. But the farmhouse was primitive beyond belief.

We had lunch in a charmingly wooded dell within sight and sound of running water. Cheerful-looking farmhands thought nothing of roasting a whole sheep for us over a fire of sticks and dried camel dung. The dung gave off clouds of thick, evil smelling blue smoke which made my eyes water. Hikmet Bey explained it was good for keeping mosquitoes away. The dung is gathered by the women employed on the farm, dried in flat rounds and stacked ingeniously so that the air can circulate freely. After we had filled ourselves with lamb which, camel dung or no camel dung, had never tasted so good, we were served with bowls of sheep's-milk yoghurt, very thick and sour. Hikmet Bey, bursting with pride, pointed out his sheep to me on a nearby hill. They looked like balls of cotton wool.

The afternoon was hot but Hikmet Bey was indefatigable. He was proud and boastful, and Dursun Bey and I followed him wearily, less interested in all the scientific wonders he had to show us than in finding some cool spot to rest.

The pale gold of the wheat shimmered in the heat and distant hills seemed to swim in a faint grey mist. The work of the farm was orderly, progressive and a triumph of endurance in that near-tropical weather. Men and women of all ages were working in the fields, in the orchards and the sheds. I was staggered by their industry. Many of them slept in the fields during the summer months, since the fields were often a great distance from the shacks they called home.

Under a so-called democratic regime, Hikmet Bey lived like a sultan, the peasants bent double making money for him. Whether he treated them well or not there was no knowing in so brief a time, but I reflected that it was rather shocking to see the fine stalls, sluices and elaborate milking equipment provided for the cows, while the workers lived in mud huts. Yet they were probably better off like this than trying to wrest a living by themselves, for with Hikmet Bey's protection they at least ensured the safe harvesting of their own meagre crops.

Despite the fact that they lived comparatively close to a town as large as Konya, they were simpler and more withdrawn than many peasants I was to meet in other parts of Anatolia. This may have been due to the vastness of Hikmet Bey's farm, which allowed them less independence. They were as compact and as close mouthed as any tightly knit little community can be. Some of them owned a few fields, a donkey, perhaps a goat, but these alone would never have supported them, and it was to Hikmet Bey they turned for the necessities of life.

It was obvious they were proud of having such a progressive man in their midst. One young man, his face and neck tanned to the colour of old leather, pointed to the reaper and binder with pride. Others made attempts to initiate me into the mysteries of a tractor. I am not mechanically minded, however, and its advantages were wasted on me. I asked one young farmhand, a married man with two small children, if he wouldn't be better off with a job in Konya. He replied that if he went to Konya there would be no one to look after his few acres of land and the half-dozen or so sheep which Hikmet Bey let him graze on the hill. Besides, he told me shrewdly, if he lived in Konya he would have to pay rent for a house, and he might never see a bit of meat. Here he had enough meat to eat, for now and then when Hikmet Bey came to stay at the farm he would give a sheep to the men to be roasted.

'But isn't the school a long way for your children to walk?' I asked.

'It's the same distance now as it always was,' he retorted. 'I had to walk there winter or summer and they can do the same thing. Besides, if they're clever, they can have a farm like Hikmet Bey Efendi's one day. I am better off than my father was. I went to school and I can read and write.'

On the surface, at least, all the other people I talked to seemed to feel the same. Some of them spoke proudly of sons who had done so well at primary school that at the age of twelve they had been accepted at a village institute to continue their education.

These village institutes, a direct outcome of Kemal Atatürk's policy for education, are interesting experiments. Any bright child on reaching the age of twelve, the age when compulsory education ceases in Turkey, can elect to attend a village institute. Here they are taught every aspect of village life. For six years they study the needs of villages, the care of animals – even the care of sick people – and more efficient methods of food production. During their six years of study they are separated into two classes – the children who will take up positions as teachers in village primary schools and those who wish to study for a trade. Those trained as teachers are obliged to contract themselves to work for the government for twenty-five years. The students who prefer to take up a trade are taught carpentry, bricklaying and so on. But a reasonably high percentage of institute pupils are born with the love of the land in them and these graduate to agricultural colleges, forestry schools – even a university.

As opposed to the men who spoke in favour of continued education, however, there were the diehards who maintained that education was ruining the country. One middle-aged man said that education had only taught him to lose his belief in Islam, another said that schools run by a *hoca* were the best. All of them were pleased that religious instruction had now become part of every school's curriculum.

The strength of Islam dies hard and it is in the country places that this is particularly noticeable. A *hoca*, whether of the old school or the new – the latter meaning, simply, that he has been trained under government control and is appointed by the Ministry of Religious Affairs – is more sought after when visiting a village than any head of state. The people yearn to be told that they are in danger of eternal damnation unless they mend their sinful ways. The more the *hoca* makes them visualise the fires of Hell, the more do they approve of him.

It was arranged that we should spend the night at the farm, and towards evening we visited the chicken-runs to select our dinner. Our appearance set up an agitated speculation among the hens, who left off admiring the antics of a cock and fluttered nervously in all directions. The cock, a fine specimen with a gaudy comb and iridescent wing feathers, decided that discretion was the better part of valour and flew off to a zinc roof, where he landed with a good deal of clatter and an indignant squawk. The roof, however, was far too close to where we were standing for his continued safety, and in order to reach a point where he would be out of our reach, he had to pass in front of us. This operation depended, obviously, on speed. He shivered miserably, a picture of the most abject terror, but with a sort of desperate courage he flung himself suicidally to the ground and half running, half flying reached the hens, who puffed out their chests and forced him out into the open. He was pathetic, all dignity gone, although the very next moment he had regained his conceit and was showing off to another batch of hens who had wandered over to see what all the fuss was about. Alas, his reprieve was not to be, for Hikmet Bey called a farmhand and told him to catch him, as well as one other gaudy fellow he pointed out.

Two young farmhands joined in the chase, catching the first fellow we had seen with little difficulty, for he was so busy showing off to the ladies that his doom was upon him before he realised it. However, the second bird was not to be taken by surprise. Alerted by the untimely capture of his comrade, he flew off to safety. This was an illusion, however, for a farmhand came up behind him and he missed death by inches. Fluttering wildly, he flew down to the ground and tore round and round the yard in a frenzy. The farmhands, enjoying the game, started closing in on him, and once again he took to mad flight, slithering ungracefully before he took off. He alighted, out of breath and madness in his eyes, close to Hikmet Bey who lunged forward to catch him. Hikmet Bey slipped and the cock disappeared round the corner of a henhouse. The enemy, in the shape of a grinning farmhand, cut off his retreat and back again flew the cock, gasping for breath, very near the end of his tether, but still free. I began to wish he would remain free – impossible wish in an impossible world. Hikmet Bey, hauled to his feet, now joined in the chase. Very soon it was all over. He had captured the cock, and I still retain a sentimental memory of those beady eyes rolling in hysteria unaccompanied by even a squawk of protest.

We ate in the stone-flagged kitchen of the farmhouse, where candles stood in saucers were too feeble to illuminate shadowed corners. Drinking vast quantities of *rakı*, as if it were water, Hikmet Bey grew amorous and called in some of the labourers to drink with us. The candle-light flickered on dark faces and tattered shirts. Hikmet Bey fondled a good-looking young man with a mouth as sweet as a girl's. Dursun Bey looked faintly shocked. I longed for a camera to photograph that ring of dusky faces which, loosened by *rakı* and the suggestiveness of love, was assuming a primitiveness as exciting as a Rimsky-Korsakov suite.

Someone produced a small drum and an *ud* – a five-stringed instrument shaped like a half-pear – and presently the deep throbbing rhythm of a fast Anatolian peasant tune broke on the air. A voice took up the tune, feet tapped in appreciation. The singer was a youth of about twenty, a slender, womanish figure with large dark eyes. Hikmet Bey, twisting in his chair, groaned his appreciation, and the singer's voice grew low and sweet, teasing Hikmet Bey's emotions. The thrumming of the *ud*, the dull noise of stamping feet on the earth floor, the singer's voice, all made a dark pattern on the senses of something half as old as time itself. The flickering candles highlighted lips and jutting noses, the skin stretched tautly across high Asiatic cheekbones, and the jewel-like liquidity of a dark eye. There was a sharp smell of stale sweat.

As the first song ended another broke out – the singer this time a heavy-jowled, clownish man who sang of life and death, the futility of one and the inevitability of the other. His voice was cracked and broken and should have made a parody of the song but, instead, it was made ineffably nostalgic by very reason of the voice's unevenness and the half-witted creature who sang it. It was a moment when one became aware of the true cruelty of life, when one turned away, sickened, from the oafish face and the infantile mind in the body of a grown man. The others encouraged him relentlessly, mocking his withered brain and telling dirty stories at his expense about his prowess with the village women. And all the time he laughed, glad to be the centre of attraction, boasting in a high babyish whine that he was twice as strong as most men so needed twice as many women. While he was talking, I was fascinated to watch the play of his powerful hands. They gestured roughly, thrusting themselves brutally upwards to emphasise an obscene point, the large knuckles highlighted by the candlelight, the hairy wrists as powerful as a prizefighter's.

After a time the men grew tired of baiting him, and he sulked in a corner, hidden from view, but fumblingly groping for a young boy who was plying him with *rakı*.

A boy of perhaps fifteen was pushed into the centre of the floor. His fresh adolescence was a touching thing in that stale old room. His face was tender as a dawn sky and touched with the humility of the mountain Turk, yet his eyes were already alive with the experience of living. He singled me out for his attentions, standing so close in front of me that I was aware of the little pulse beating in his throat and his head outlined in flaring candlelight. He stared at me for a moment, his eyes taunting me, then he flung back his head in laughter. He leaned forward to snatch my hand and kiss it, and all the time his lightning gaze flashed from my ring to the gold watch on my wrist. Hikmet Bey pulled him close to plant a kiss on his upturned mouth, then said thickly that he was to dance.

For a few moments the boy stood slackly, but one felt the ripple of excitement that went through the watching men. For a little longer the boy timed his movements against the beat of the music, little hesitant movements that were suggestive of young amorous limbs. Then he began to dance, carefully, painstakingly – almost clumsily – keeping in perfect time with the quickening music. His smooth young face was as blank as a sleepwalker's. He weaved a pattern with his feet, but his mind was somewhere else. His artistry was superb, for the movements of his body and the fluttering hands portrayed unmistakably a young girl's first reluctance to physical love, her gradual desire to experience it, finally her surrender.

There was no sound at all in the room save the whispering beat of the music and the slithering of the boy's feet across the floor. Men sat in rapt attention, light running silver down the side of a face or the jutting archipelago of a nose. The half-darkness was rapacious and secretive and all eyes were directed to the boy who swayed in moaning rapture, his dark shadow leaping up the wall behind him – monstrous, gigantic. The music rose and fell, offbeat, infinitely sad, for it spoke of passing earthly joys. The languorous boy stood quite still in the middle of a twirl, one foot poised above the other, the posture sustained magnificently, then, in time to the quickened music, abandoned himself to the consummation. Now his feet flew so fast I was hardly able to distinguish one from the other. His shadow leaped and jerked up the wall. His hands yearned, taut, delicate, infinitely sensuous. The climax came with violence. His low sad cry of surrender echoed round the startled room, and then he flung himself to the floor, twitching.

With the ending of the dance cries rose from dark corners where men sat clasping their hands between their thighs, lost, abandoned to the erotic moment. Someone shouted, 'All–ah,' unable to contain himself any longer. Only the musicians played on unmoved, for they were caught up in their own particular rapture. I found the experience of that night both moving and chilling, an experience so primitive that it could not fail to stir the blood, yet so expressive of man's lower nature, so imprisoning, that one felt brushed by the Devil himself.

The room was full of *rakı* fumes, of sweating humanity and the queer acrid odour of the copulations of older men. To stagger out to the sweet night air was a form of relief, for unless one has lost one's senses in drink it is impossible not to be appalled by licentiousness. Dursun Bey came out to stand beside me, and together we looked out at the dark outline of the hills and the villages that lay sleeping at their feet.

'I could have gone outside with that boy,' he said to me regretfully. 'You know, he looked at me many times.'

I was moved again by the memory of the dancer and the certainty that he would never grow old.

The moon was high in the sky, infinitely remote, symbol of men's dreams. Trees stood out on the horizon like a frieze. In my mind's eye I saw, as in a witch's ball, the figure of myself, spellbound.

4

A Model Village – Islamic Customs – Camels –
More about the Yürük – Talking Politics

THE NEXT DAY Hikmet Bey, recovered from the previous night's orgy, drove us to a village a few kilometres beyond Meram. This was because I had expressed interest in seeing a go-ahead village.

The village of Muradköy at first sight presented a picture of hard-working orderliness, a tidy village of little over one thousand people, large by Turkish village standards.

We passed vineyards on the way which looked dry and neglected, although Hikmet Bey said that this wasn't really so. The apparent air of neglect was due to the excessively hot spring and summer, which had ruined more than half the grapes, and the speed with which the people had had to work to recover those that were marketable. Presently, he said, when the time was right, the workers would be back again and the vines would be pruned and so on.

There was a newly built mosque in the village and a primary school of raw red brick. In winter the roads were still lakes of mud but the *muhtar*, a reasonable man, said that this state of affairs was being attended to. They couldn't run before they walked, he said, and already they had achieved a great deal. He was firmly on the side of the Democrats. The school, which we were shown over, was certainly ambitious for a village. Three teachers had been assigned to it, and there was provision for two hundred pupils between the ages of seven and twelve.

The Menderes government, aiming to enlarge the rural vote, had brought water to the village, and some of the more prosperous villagers had this laid on in their houses. There was a mill as well, where the community wheat was ground at very little cost. This was not always made use of, however, for the peasants still liked to take their wheat to the mill in another village, where they had always gone previously. The other mill charged less and the peasants preferred to make a longer journey rather than part with a few extra hard-earned *kuruş*.

The people were cheerful, and well pleased with what the Democrat government was doing for them. A little over eight per cent of the villagers owned from five to forty acres of land, another ten per cent owned from three to five acres, and the rest worked on farms or on government projects. Muradköy was fortunate, of course, in being within reasonable distance of Konya and two market towns, where once a week produce was taken in carts with iron rimmed-wheels. Everyone I spoke to seemed optimistic. A young man who worked his own land said he hoped I wouldn't give a false picture of peasant life to my friends.

'We are a progressive nation,' he said proudly, 'and we have come a long way in little over a quarter of a century. There are people who would like to believe we are as backward as our fathers were, but it isn't so. We have everything we want, thank God, and we would like everyone to know it.'

He spat contemptuously, angry because he had been questioned.

An older man, however, had a different tale to tell.

'We're the same as we always were,' he said. 'We only send our children to school because we're afraid of the *jandarma*. A new school is built and a mosque, but that doesn't put bread in our stomachs. We work hard and we live hard. Anyone who tells you we're progressive wants his head examined. You can't judge us by coming here and asking a lot of silly questions. You'd need to live among us, see what we have to eat and the way the children go to bed hungry on a winter's night. That would show you how much we've changed, so don't run away with the idea that you know anything about village life just by looking at us on a summer's day.'

The houses were one storey, built of *kerpiç*, which is a mixture of mud and straw, but many of them were neatly whitewashed. I saw only two brick-built houses, and these looked as raw and out of place as the new school. Despite the warnings of the villagers to whom I had spoken, I was still impressed with the village. Before the Republic there would have been no school, and no smallholders. Nowadays, two families owned tractors, another a reaper, and several possessed other farm implements. And as well as the blaring coffee-shop radio, there were a score of others in the houses. Most of the women said they owned a sewing machine and all of them wore huge gold bracelets about their wrists, investments for a rainy day perhaps.

Their diet was simple to the point of nauseousness. Breakfast consisted of a cereal soup with black bread. The midday meal might be dried haricot beans cooked with onions, bread and sheep's-milk yoghurt made by the woman of the house. *Pekmez*, a heavy grape syrup, was drunk in preference to water, although the year I was there there was very little *pekmez* owing to the effects of the drought. Sometimes the midday meal would be varied by adding a dish of potatoes, but this sort of luxury was generally reserved for weekends. The last meal of the day was *pilav* (made from bleached wheat, however, and not from rice) or macaroni boiled in bone water. Fresh vegetables were scarce and expensive. *Turşu* was made by the women from red cabbage, golden cucumbers or red peppers, with salt and dill water added.

Politics held little interest for them – unless some government decree touched them directly. If this were favourable, they showed their pleasure by praising the government. If it was unfavourable they spoke their mind to the *muhtar* – although they had to be careful about this for a previous *muhtar* had had a nasty habit of entering as a Communist anyone who disagreed with government policy. The moment he communicated his views to the police, the unfortunate villager was arrested, and who was to prove whether he was a Communist or not? Nobody cared. The accused was thrown into prison and left to rot, and no one would help his family for fear of being thought to have Communist sympathies.

The yearly conscription of the young men was the ever festering sore. Old men complained of crops being left in the fields to rot because the army had taken their sons. A widow I spoke to had had, the previous winter, to be kept by the charity of her neighbours and what little work she could get to do in the fields, because her son had been taken away from her and there was nobody to support her. The government does not give any money to the dependants of soldiers.

The *muhtar*, who seemed to be an earnest and conscientious man, said that the people of his village were better off than they had ever been. A government doctor visited them twice a year and hospitalisation was free. Cholera and dysentery, once the curse of this area, were now virtually unheard of. Malaria had decreased, and the people themselves were beginning to take an interest in the hygienic measures laid down by the government. He admitted that taxation still came as a heavy burden, but at least, he said, there was no more forced labour or deportation to some other part of the country on government work if the people were not able to meet tax demands immediately.

Religion burned as fiercely as ever, kept alive from the cradle to the grave by the example of parents, by customs and habits and, of course, by the fact that all schools devote a certain amount of time to religious instruction. Even the very young heeded the call of the muezzin. Bodily cleanliness, as integral a part of Islam as fasting or praying, is taught to the youngest child. Pubic hair and hair under the arms is regarded as unclean; the Christian use of toilet paper instead of water is considered the very depths of uncleanliness. The posterior, associated with filth, must be washed with the left hand only, consequently food should never be touched with the left hand. A husband and wife must not make love before washing their private parts; neither may they sleep without cleansing themselves afterwards. This may be regarded as a common-place in Western countries but in a land where the problem of water is ever present, it had to be laid down as a religious rule. Nobody enters the mosque without washing his feet, and donning clean underwear – providing he can afford the latter. Adolescent boys whose penises are constantly erect cannot enter a mosque in this state but must content themselves with praying in their homes. This, of course, calls attention to their plight, but nobody seems to feel any embarrassment.

Religious *bayram* are occasions for fasting and prayer as well as rejoicing. The rich people who can afford the pilgrimage to Mecca are held in great respect. Water blessed at Mecca is part of the healing equipment of every household, and the Muslim rosary of thirty-three beads is an equally treasured possession. The name of God is invoked a thousand times in a day, yet cruelty to children, to animals and to each other is not an abnormal pattern of behaviour. Sexual aberrations are pronounced. Dishonesty, infidelity, even murder, are unaffected by religious belief. Because the peasant is unable to identify himself with animals, his cruelty is childlike and often irresponsible. A dying dog is kicked into a ditch; a hen with its head half severed, an occasion for laughter. Islam teaches charity and compassion, but the majority of villagers have seen neither and the words are mere ciphers.

I do not know if peasant women have yet acquired souls; it is doubtful, for women are still regarded as chattels. The few peasant girls who benefit from advanced education, who make something of their lives in the cities or towns and who marry from choice, are so much in the minority as to have no effect at all on the ones who are left in the villages.

It seemed to me that Westernisation affected the villager only in so far as it gave him farm machinery (not infrequently left in the fields to rust), schools, civic rights and other much favoured amenities. All these, of course, are external things. They leave no mark on his spirit, which is still brutal, insensitive and tragic. The whole of village life in Anatolia is tragic. One has only to look into the eyes of the children or the long-suffering women. Life seems to be an unremitting struggle with nature or against people more worldly than themselves who cheat them relentlessly. For all the obvious improvements, life is hard in the village. It will remain so for a long time to come, until the people themselves begin to appreciate that there *is* a finesse to living at all.

In Muradköy – not a collection of mud huts, after all – I was reminded of how close they still are to nomadism. This is shown in their lack of civic interest, their houses which are equipped with the barest necessities of life, their zest for the open air and their acceptance of long journeys to market or elsewhere which, despite what anyone opines, they do not complain about. It is as though the long jog into town, either on foot or on a sleepy donkey, sets their spirits free. For centuries they have lived in near squalor, as though settled by accident on one spot of ground which they will never call their own. Their lives are without romance, yet in their music and their dancing they often strew stars at their feet.

When the day's work is done the old men meet at the coffee-house for discussion, the women sit under a plane tree knitting, gossiping, chattering as though they hadn't a care in the world. One family I heard of even slept in the open all the summer, giving up their house to the snakes that had invaded it for coolness.

The children are grave – indeed, all Turkish children are grave; it seems to be a national characteristic. They play solemn little games with a ball or fly home-made kites. Poor feeding results in listlessness. Only the camel caravans are able to arouse enthusiasm. 'The camels have been many days on the road already,' one small boy told me, and his yearning eyes followed them, these purveyors of all their dreams, these heroic men and camels who live on the road and not in a house.

I must confess that the camel caravans stirred me too, so perhaps no Turk ever loses his nomadic instincts. They spelled the last romantic survival in a commercialised world of noise and petrol fumes. It is true that the camels were generally ugly brutes with dun-coloured hides and yellowed teeth. I think it was their unbelievable eyelashes that gave them some touching quality. They heaved and groaned, pulling back their rubbery lips in futile anger, yet when they had their proud heads erect and gazed at one mournfully, one was instantly wounded by the childish eyelashes and the look of sorrow in their eyes. Hikmet Bey said this was all moonshine. They knew neither sorrow nor joy. I clung to my belief, however, and when one of the men showed me a young camel foal and I caught its soft face in my hands, my heart was squeezed by the look of patience in the velvety eyes.

I could well understand the small boys who declared they would be camel drivers when they grew up – just as a child in another country says he will be an engine driver, for who cannot see romance in the camel caravans? And in the long journeyings from one end of a country to the borders of another, climbing the inhospitable mountains, following interminable trails – laid centuries ago – along the feet of the Taurus Mountains, threading the shallows of the Euphrates, winding between the black rocks of Diyarbakır, straining ever upwards across the fearsome Zigana Pass? One associates them with jade and amber, silks and spices; nowadays, unfortunately, they carried only salt or bales of cotton or lighter flints. They were there for all to see, real unbelievably romantic, but it was all a pretty myth; they too were touched by the commercial needs of the world.

Dursun Bey called Muradköy a show village. 'There are far worse than this in eastern Anatolia,' he said. 'Wait until you come to Diyarbakır, there I'll show you some that make this place seem like a well-run town.'

'True enough,' Hikmet Bey agreed, and pointed to Karadağ in the distance, a mountain as black and lowering as a thundercloud. 'Behind those mountains are the real primitives,' he said. 'Up on the top of Karadağ the Yürük live. They have no schools up there, no visiting doctors, no water – except what God provides for them. There are feuds and tribal law. The better man wins all the time, not necessarily the best. The Yürük people live high in the mountains and nothing much is known about them. I have heard it said they are older than our ancestors, the Selcuks. And lower down the mountains there are villages, so they say, where the land is nothing but scrub, and the forests, where they cut the wood to cart to the lowlands, are often twenty miles away from them. You people who travel in the cities see nothing.'

'Tell me something about the Yürük,' I interrupted, ignoring his jibe at surface travellers.

'Who knows them?' he countered. 'They are nomads, we all know that. They live in tents. During the summer they go higher up in the mountains for pasturage for their flocks. Perhaps they live much as our ancestors lived when first they found their way to Anatolia. They have their own dialect, I'm told, a language purer than our own, although recognisable as Turkish, of course. Once a year they gather in the village of Manavgat, not far from Antalya. They dress in their national costumes and make merry for three days and three nights. After their festival is over they return to their tents where birds never fly and camels cannot pass.'

'I should like to go there,' I said.

Hikmet Bey laughed at me. 'You'd never come back alive,' he said. 'You're too soft for that sort of life.'

However, I was determined to get there. I knew not how, but that didn't matter for the moment. My imagination was stirred.

Before leaving Muradköy, we dined with the *muhtar*, who frowned when I mentioned the Yürük people and said he knew nothing about them. He would discuss nothing but the progress his village was making and the impressive plans that were to be carried out in the following year. He spoke of the Halk Partisi with contempt, declaring they had done nothing for the country. I am not in favour of any political party in Turkey, and have never had very definite ideas on this score, but I was saddened at the fate of Atatürk's companions who had, after all, started the country on the road to Westernisation.

We drove back to Hikmet Bey's home in brilliant moonlight. We were alone on the silver road. Once Hikmet Bey stopped the car and said 'Listen!' and we listened to the silence ringing in our ears. Then a jackal started to cry in the hills. The inhuman voice was strangely chilling at that lonely hour, and might have been a ferine baby crying. From Muradköy, far behind us, came the barking of a dog. A bat flew across the moon.

'Frightening, isn't it?' I said.

'And yet wonderful,' said Hikmet Bey. 'When I was abroad I missed the voice of the country. I couldn't hurry home quickly enough.'

'I have never been farther from home than this,' said Dursun Bey.

I thought how far away I was from the place I called 'home' and wondered if a time would ever come when I would settle down willingly and for ever. It seemed an impossible thought. I am always happy on the move.

We arrived to find Hikmet Bey's home in darkness, which caused him to curse his wife who, he said, had been expecting him back. We groped our way along the broken path and Dursun Bey struck matches now and then, which did no more than dazzle the eye, making darkness infinitely darker.

Our arrival caused all the dogs to bark and half the household to descend in their nightclothes. Lamps were lit and food prepared, and Hikmet Bey's wife – whom we had heard, not seen – retired to bed again. We three sat on for a little longer in the over-furnished *salon*, talking of this and that, tired but unwilling to make the effort to go to bed.

Hikmet Bey, who had been a member of parliament until the defeat of the Halk Partisi in 1950, spoke highly of the *muhtar* with whom we had dined.

'But have you lost all interest in politics?' I asked, amazed at such charity, remembering especially all the bitter things that had been said over dinner.

'I have no time for politics,' he replied.

Dursun Bey, already half asleep, stirred and said: 'Who'd want to have anything to do with politics these days? The papers are muzzled.'

'The papers have been muzzled ever since we have had the Republic, and even before that,' I answered.

'Well,' Hikmet Bey observed testily, 'there's no need for us to talk about all that now. Everything in the country is in the hands of a few people in Ankara, who build silos that are never used, buy machinery that rusts in the depots – or the fields, it's all one – and is happier pulling down cities than rebuilding villages. They have made us, or will make us, an American outpost, but who's to do anything about it? The national debt is over four hundred million pounds sterling and going higher, and it's the devil's own job to live at all. But what's so odd about any of it, except that we're trying to fool the world and ourselves? It was as bad in the previous government's time, I'll admit that, and in Atatürk's time, and in the Sultan's before him. As long as they leave me alone, I'm content. I tell you, I'm sick of politics.'

5

Hikmet Bey arranges an Expedition – Karaman –
My Adventurous Ancestor – Amateur Mountaineers –
Alevi v. Sunni – Phantoms of the Night

THE YÜRÜK fascinated me. The more I heard about them, the more determined I was to visit them. Hikmet Bey constantly discouraged me. 'Nobody within living memory has gone up Karadag and lived to tell the tale,' he would say, ominously.

Yet my desire persisted and, firing him with my own enthusiasm, I soon had the phlegmatic Dursun Bey on my side. Hikmet Bey weakened as far as saying he would make enquiries from his farm manager.

It was difficult to learn much about the Yürük. Books made no mention of them, beyond the fact that they existed and were nomadic, and local people were vague and uninterested. However, from the picture we were able to build up, albeit shadowy and incomplete, the Yürük emerged, timeless and touched with mystery.

They are descended from the Oguz tribes who came out of Central Asia in the sixth century. They live in the mountains all over Turkey, scattered, cut off from civilisation. Ertuğrul, father of Osman who founded the Ottoman Dynasty, is their hero, and since the day of his death, seven hundred and thirty years ago, they gather once a year at Söğüt, where his tomb is. The day they choose is the 9th of March, which is the spring festival.

The long trek to Söğüt is made by donkey and camel. The Yürük wear the traditional embroidered costumes of their tribes, identical with those worn by their ancestors over a thousand years before them. This gathering is both a pilgrimage and a festival – the one to honour Ertugrul the other to salute the spring. They make a gay procession, carrying flags, beating drums, thrumming out a fast rhythm on the *zurna*. From all over Turkey they converge on the little town of Söğüt, but before their festivities begin they go in solemn procession to pay their respects to Ertuğrul. Gathered round his unpretentious tomb, they pray noisily then attend a special service at the mosque. The serious business over, they commence their merrymaking. Wrestling contests are held, sword fights, dancing contests, and so on.

They set their camps outside the town. The women prepare whole roasted lambs and mountains of snowy *pilav*. The children and the young girls dance and sing, while the sporting young men leap around them, showing off their physical prowess. The women are as wild and free as birds and have never known the restriction of veil or *çarşaf*.

After whetting our appetites for several more days, Hikmet Bey one morning announced that he was ready to accompany us to the mountains. He said that his farm manager knew of a reliable guide. I was overjoyed, but Dursun Bey began to have misgivings. Supposing, he said, we never returned … ? But it is extraordinary how little this means in the face of adventure. The thought of death remains shadowy, an experience to be met by someone else, never oneself.

The day before we left, I went out into the country alone. A mood of solitude had descended upon me, as dark and soft as a moth's wings. On every horizon mountains unfolded in a series of undulating curves. The sun beat down with all its force on the rocky peaks which rose up against an exhausted sky. The brilliance of the light dazzled and blurred the vision. The day was still as eternity and only the grass, dotted with the wild flowers of the upland summer, whispered in the small breeze of my passing. Away in the distance, like a voice out of nowhere, a tinkle of sheep bells could be heard. The road sloped into a valley, and here too the rays of the sun were beating down with merciless force.

Down by a small stream a heron fished, a solemn pale-grey bird with the surprised eyes of a virgin caught at her toilet. Beyond the valley I came out on a dusty road, full of afternoon shadows and slanting light. There was the rich solitude of the trees and the scents of the country – as if incense had been scattered on the air. There was a wooden bridge with no handrails over a river and, beyond, a village of mud huts where heavy plane trees hung out over the water. A few children played in a dusty clearing; a woman was washing clothes at the river's edge, beating them against a stone. The blue smoke of camel dung rose waveringly against a paler sky. The village lay sheltered by the wooded hills, asleep; the young men and girls worked in the orchards on the other side of the valley. A grove of trees stood with their heads together, in the centre of them a dead grey skeleton that at some time past had been struck by lightning. The trees looked old, their bright green heads' sly semblance of youth only a deception, for their roots curled in and out of the cracked earth around them like serpents. They were hard primitive roots in sunburned earth, enormously old.

I leaned against an ancient tree watching the murmur of life around me, and it seemed as if the whole glowing landscape might at any moment dissolve, leaving me looking down through layer after layer of mist into the transparencies of time. The whole valley, enveloped in mosses and lichens, looked old beyond time. The ticking watch went by unheeded here. It was as unheeded as the sun, the wind and the rain, and more temporal. In such a setting it seemed absurd to pay too much attention to the things that were still engulfed in time, the conferences and speeches of little men still taking place beyond this timeless valley. Here, in this scorched village, life went on in slow motion, in a pattern of brilliant simplicity, subtly renouncing the world and surrounded with stillness like a mirror, close – but unapproachable – and I knew that the longing to return, to be engulfed in this primitive consciousness, would remain with me forever.

The woman beside the river finished beating out her clothes, the children caught sight of me and ran into a hut, whence presently a dog issued barking. I turned back up the valley to where, crowning the summit above me, high up in the sparkling sunlight, were two quiet groves of olive trees. They were alive and radiant, growing with the quiet mystery that has passed even beyond time itself and is lost in the womb of the world.

It was late when I climbed down to the main road again and evening closed around me, trailing amethyst mists. Distant trees were bowed with shadow and in the east the mountains were already black. I remembered that tomorrow we would be on Karadağ.

That night we dined on the terrace under little coloured lamps which had been fixed in the overhanging vines. We had *patlican karni-yarık*, young aubergines filled with meat and herbs and slices of tomato steeped in red wine; chicken *pilav*; green peppers stuffed with rice and wild chicory; and melons served on ice. We toasted each other in *rakı*, and all the time there was a vision before my eyes. The ancient land enfolded me, seeping down to the very roots of my being, so that past and present seemed indivisible and I was carried along, helpless, enchanted by time, which stood ever at my shoulder.

That night Hikmet Bey's character came into its own. He told of the plans he had made, of the precautions he had taken. Like a good general he came up with alternatives, never at a loss for a word. Listening to him, I had the feeling that we were going into some vast hinterland from which we might never return – or return transmuted, purged of all longing and desire ever to travel again. Indeed, he made Karadağ seem some impossibly far-off place, the traversing of which might be fraught with high adventure – a journey that necessitated vast food stocks, well-oiled revolvers and nerves of steel. To us, looking out across the moonlit terrace, Karadağ seemed near enough to touch; impossible to believe it might harbour death.

Down by the pool where the ducks waddled by day, the weeping willows were bright like waterfalls. Between pools of shadow moonlight lay richly on the broken flagstones. Above the distant hills were flashes of rose-coloured lightning and the stillness of the night presaged storm.

Hikmet Bey's wife packed food for us, and a change of shirt and shoes in our rucksacks. She hovered nervously, running into the house to shelter each time there was a growl of thunder in the distance. The thunder grew nearer, the lightning became more frequent, and presently a few heavy drops of rain pattered down through the leaves above our heads.

I went into the house reluctantly, for the coming storm had made tension mount in me like a tightly-coiled spring. Now the rain lashed down with the fury of tropical intensity, flinging itself on the roof and shaking the leaves in the garden. We could hear it splashing on the terrace. It seeped through the closed doors, seeming to invade the house itself. Once the lights threatened to go out, and the women crept in to where we were, frightened, their heads – even at this late hour – muffled by scarves. Presently the rain grew quieter. Now it flowed and dripped against the walls with a sound like someone crying, someone whose sighs were drifting through the drenched trees. The thunder receded gradually into the black depths of the night and soon there was only the steady pattering of the rain. After a time, this too ceased and the silence weighed on the mind like eternity.

I opened the door, looking down the damp garden where everything still swayed a little, as though not yet recovered from the wild onslaught of the storm. Little puddles glistened. Thunder still sounded from far away, but overhead, in rifts in the clouds, the moon flashed and a few bright stars peered down inquisitively at the tossed earth.

It was drizzling when we left next morning, with a hard grey sky promising heavier rain later. This seemed a depressing start and we grumbled as we shrugged ourselves into raincoats we had not thought to need. Hikmet Bey cursed fluently and consistently, for his raincoat was of gaberdine, too hot for the time of the year. I had a plastic one I had bought in Izmir and felt smug.

Rain clouds drowned the peak of Karadağ. The horizon was flat, unfamiliar, infinitely inimical to our plans. The women of the house complicated matters still further by begging us to delay our journey for another day, prophesying bad luck and the mischief of jinn if we undertook our adventure in this weather. Such counsel only made Hikmet Bey swear all the more, for Hikmet Bey is a modern man and has no use for old wives' tales. I, who am made of much less stern stuff, wondered uneasily if there might not be something in what they said.

We drove off into the rainy dawn, our eyes sleep rimmed. I patted my revolver and tried to feel like a hero setting out on some great adventure; instead of which I felt like a middle-aged man who needed more sleep. Hikmet Bey, huddled over the wheel, and Dursun Bey, dozing beside me, were the epitome of disinterestedness. We bumped over a rickety bridge; puddles still glistened on the roads after last night's storm.

The whole landscape was drained of colour; flat and desolate, it stretched away before us, with low clouds hiding the hills. The sky was immense, a sheet of steel that threatened to engulf us. Rain drove, in spiteful little jerks, against the windows of the car, and I turned up my collar trying to evade the drops that came in through the tops of the insecure windows. A flock of wild duck fanned out overhead, their white bodies heavy with rain. They were the only signs of life in that grey wilderness. I was filled with despair. I wanted to ask Hikmet Bey to turn back. The sun and dreams of yesterday were forgotten. I was suspended in a vacuum of misery and the empty landscape was utterly without sympathy.

We bumped over rough tracks, and every time we bumped a little splatter of raindrops forced their way through the window on my side, striking against my face or, more insidiously, finding their way down my neck. We reached the farm at last where hot coffee revived us and drove away the last lingering remnants of sleep.

My spirits began to revive. The farm manager was affable, and rain or no rain, men were staggering about the yard with sacks and bundles, cheerfully active. Our guide was produced – a tall, powerfully built man called Cemal, who shared our breakfast of coarse farm bread, olives and white cheese. He radiated energy and a disregard for the weather that made our raincoats and our preoccupation with shoes and supplies of *gripin* effeminate and unnecessary. He had spent the whole of his life between Meram, Kavakli and Karaman, and had no desire to go farther afield. His eyes lit up and his grizzled face looked young, almost tender, when he spoke of the mountains, where from the age of seven he had guarded sheep or herded goats. He was inarticulate when it came to talking about himself, but one could see he was a man who loved solitude. Looking out across the wet trees, he said it would be fine in another hour or so. The sun would be so hot we would find it stiff going up Karadağ, and he looked at us with a fugitive pity – three city gents in search of adventure.

We asked him what he knew about the Yürük people, but he was unable to tell us anything we didn't already know – except that they didn't take kindly to strangers invading their ancestral ground. He had once been high up on Karadağ, searching for sheep, when he came upon their tents, but that was the only contact he had had with them.

The sky showed signs of clearing and Cemal said we ought to be off. He knew of a semi-nomadic village, halfway up Karadağ, where we could spend the night. He shouldered our rucksacks and remarked that our shoes didn't look as if they'd stand up to much climbing. Subdued, feeling like children reproved by an elder, we looked at our handsome shoes which we had bought in Konya in the belief that these were what mountaineers wore.

'It isn't so much that you're going to climb a mountain,' said Cemal patiently, 'but that the heat will kill you, and your backs will be broken.'

The farm manager came round with the horses that were to take us as far as Karaman, where they were to be left at another outpost of Hikmet Bey's great farm. They were graceful little mares with flowing tails and they whinnied their desire to be off. They lifted their elegant heads, widening their nostrils and prancing impatiently about us. Conscious of my shoes, I should have liked them to take us all the way.

It was good to be in the saddle again, to let the mare have her head and feel the morning breeze on one's face. I began to enjoy myself, and the good feel of horseflesh under me added zest to the journey. I galloped away ahead of the others, the wanton mare as delighted as I was, and the sun, choosing just this moment to scatter the clouds, signified his approval of the whole thing. We dropped to a walk, letting the others catch up with us, and as I reined in, waiting for them to come alongside me, the little mare flung up her head, whinnying because her freedom had been so short lived. There is something about a horseman that is time-less and the three coming to meet me might have been out of any age. The clip-clop of a horse's hooves is sweeter than any other sound I know.

The landscape was empty of life. Meram's orchards were far behind us and here there was nothing but untilled land and bare hills. It was hot already, and the wet trees steamed, little clouds of mist rising up all round us. The whole scene had a dreamlike quality, a magic that deceived the eye as well as the heart, and I wanted to ride on forever with my three silent companions into an unknown country where noise and the fret of civilisation had no power. The sun and the wet earth mingled, producing hot, resinous scents. A bird flew out of a thicket, surprised at our sudden appearance. The horses tossed their heads, harness jingling, and picked their way delicately, avoiding the rapidly drying puddles and the boulders that were strewn everywhere.

We reached Karaman all too soon, watching regretfully as the mares were led away by a labourer. We had been kings for such a short time.

Karaman is the heart of the Selcuk country, a flaming plateau bleached by the sun. There are trees everywhere, tall poplars that guard the dusty roads and plane trees that dip their heads in gossip above small white houses and the courtyards of mosques. Rising among them are the russet brown domes and minarets, the crumbled walls and gateways of the Selcuk warriors. The pale colours of broken tiles flashed in the sunlight – blue, green and shades of sapphire. Coupled with the green of the trees and the wide expanse of deeper sky they give Karaman the quality and feel of a Persian landscape.

Frowned on by my companions, I wasted precious time wandering through the ruins of the mosques. The courtyards were silent, the fountains useless, choked with lichens and weeds. Fragments of tiles surviving on a gateway were a triumph of art, with carved arabesques of leaves and flowers, delicate, enduring, forgotten. The shadows of the trees made arabesques at my feet, and I touched the sunny wall, seeking to identify myself with its roughness, reflecting that it was as warm to my hand as it had ever been to the Selcuk who had built it. And deep in the silence, in the whispering of the tall trees and the weeds growing lush about my feet, I thought to catch the echo of dead voices, the chant of a dead muezzin, fading, elusive, mysterious, pressed back to their long sleep by inexorable time.

The rich artistry of the Selcuk princes is everywhere crumbling back to the brown earth from which it sprang, and where long ages ago animals grazed, goats were grazing again. Confined as we are within the limiting horizons of our senses, we see not the greatness of the Selcuk princes – who established a humane, settled civilisation in the midst of a semi-nomadic society – but only the shadow, the faint outline, of their achievement. Melancholy, oppression, resignation brood above the remains of the mosques they built, a motionless eternity that touches the heart for past glory.

Nomadic in spirit only, I have always nevertheless felt closer to the Selcuks than the Ottomans. This has nothing to do with Kemal Atatürk's desire that every modern Turk should identify himself with the Selcuks, whose conquerors, the Ottomans, he himself destroyed. And it is perhaps a little odd that memories of the Selcuks have such power over me, for as far as I know my history is only directly traceable from the Ottomans themselves. At least, my grandmother had a picturesque story she used to tell when we were children. This alleged that our family fortunes, which by that time we had lost forever, were founded by an adventurer named Osman, who in the year 1637 quelled a petty revolt in the east of Turkey. Summoned before the sultan, Murat IV – a man notable in history for cutting off heads – he was so terrified of having his own removed that he recited a long and splendid poem, composed on the spur of the moment, in fulsome praise of Murat. He was rewarded with a bag of gold, neglected to return to the east, and was eventually made governor of Bursa – a notable achievement – where his insignificant tomb still is.

My grandmother in her later years, an autocrat built after his own pattern, once made a pilgrimage to his tomb where, weeping and wailing over the loss of fortune and prestige, she was caught trying to chip a bit of stone off his sarcophagus. Asked for an explanation, she declared she was only taking what was, rightly speaking, her own: this was the tomb of her ancestor. Could she then, she was asked, prove royal ancestry, for this was the tomb of Sultan Osman, founder of the Ottomans. Speechless with disbelief, she was led round and round a crumbling cemetery until the tomb of Osman, the one-time governor, was found lurking and insignificant, amidst a welter of other officials. My grandmother, having exhausted her grief at the tomb of the sultan, felt she couldn't whip up any more, and left her ancestor to moulder. She scarcely ever mentioned him again.

By the time I had finished walking round the Selcuk remains, Dursun Bey was already complaining that his feet hurt. He thought it exceedingly selfish of Hikmet Bey to have denied us the horses for the trek up Karadağ. I pointed out that, apart from the horses being needed on the land, I had thought we were all agreed that to climb on foot was the essence of the adventure. He was not convinced, however, and went on grumbling.

Hikmet Bey and Cemal were discovered resting under a plane tree in what, I suppose, was the centre of Karaman. They were surrounded by small boys and old men, who appeared to be enchanted that the great Hikmet Bey was in their midst. There was a bronze bust of Atatürk on a tall pedestal, and a youth came out of the coffee shop with a brass tray of coffees round his neck. Not far away from us camels crouched in a circle, some of them being loaded with their burdens. They kept up a low grumbling which every now and then broke out into a heart-rending groan. Nobody took any notice of them, except me.

It was nearing noon when we set off again, leaving us ample time, as we thought, to reach the semi-nomadic settlement before nightfall, for Cemal was reluctant for us to be caught in the mountains in darkness.

We set off at a smart pace, swinging our sticks, and shooing off the lean hungry curs that insisted on following us. The road was stony, the going uneven, and – for my part – I kept a constant lookout for snakes. The distant Taurus Mountains, blue and splendid, were capped with snow that even from this distance looked dazzling. Karadağ itself loomed black and threatening, an ominous and romantic mountain, lifting its graceful curves from the sun-baked plain. Clouds hid its summit, and owing to a trick of light, it looked as black as its name.

After nearly three hours' gentle climbing we found, to our dismay, that we had only reached the foot of the mountain. We sat down in an uncomfortable ditch to rest and eat. Only Cemal was still in shape for walking. Dursun Bey was suffering from a blister. Cemal went off to gather dock leaves which Dursun Bey put on his heel underneath his socks. His shoes were then found to be too tight for him so he had to walk with the laces taken out. This added to his misery, but caused a good deal of juvenile hilarity among the rest of us.

We set off again, vowing to take the incline as slowly as Cemal would allow us. The path was steep and treacherously slippery with the beaten-down grass. Blossoming wild flowers were all round us and myrtle buds, looking like frozen tears, threatened our path, splaying out from the trees inquisitively. We were tired and thirsty, and Cemal began to fear for our water supply. The muscles of my back and legs were pulling, and perspiration dripped coldly down my back. We detoured round the lower, gentler slopes but never seemed to be making much upward progress. We had to rest several times because of Dursun's blister.

The scenery was breathtaking, and the profusion of bright wild flowers added gaiety. We met no one on the way. We might have been reconnoitring a dead country. Now and then great jagged outcrops of rock made us hold our breath lest Cemal suggest we try to negotiate them, and the terrors and hazards of real mountaineering began to be appreciated. For the most part, however, we followed the Yürük camel route so were in no danger of being asked to do the impossible. We began to realise what Cemal had meant about our shoes, for very soon it became apparent that they were not heavy enough. Stones bit into the soles, our feet began to swell with the heat and soon all of us, except Cemal, were minus the laces.

The sky paled with afternoon light and the sun was already heeling westwards when we came across our first village – a few shepherds' huts perched on a jagged outcrop of rock. This was the settlement Cemal had told us about, and we were glad to have made it in such good time, for within another two hours it would be dark.

The village was unbelievably primitive. A few *kerpiç* houses were built close to the earth, dogs came out to snap at our heels, and the rotting wood of the huts gave off an odour of decay. Women in shapeless clothes darted away from our sight – women who had had contact with the towns and the imprisoning *çarşaf*. Even the children were shy, creeping up on us quietly then fleeing the moment we turned to look at them. Several men stood in a group together, watching us, and making no attempt to come forward. They looked surly and, I thought, hostile. However, one of them eventually detached himself from the group and came forward to greet us.

'*Selamun-aleykum*' (Peace be upon you), he greeted us, folding his right hand over his breast, and bowing.

'*Aleykum-selam*' (And peace on you too), we replied, returning his bow.

He explained that he was the headman of the village and that we were welcome to share in his poor hospitality. But all the time his eyes went on searching, seeming to light on me more than anyone else, and I felt a hostility in him that was far from reassuring.

Thin green tea was served to us, and we were invited to rest in one of the huts. However, the dark interior, from which issued clouds of dung smoke, repelled us and we said we would prefer to stay and talk with him. His eyebrows drew together in a quick frown, although he courteously made way for us on a stone seat beside him. His companions came over to join us, one of them addressing Hikmet Bey by name.

The stone where we sat was burning hot to the touch, although the sun had gone off it some time ago. I was in no mood to remain in the village overnight, and would have preferred the freedom of the mountains to the imprisoning huts of these people, who looked capable of easy violence.

The plain lay below us, quivering still in sunlight, and I was amazed at the distance we had climbed. Another bowl of green tea was brought to us and we drank thirstily. The men did not offer us any food, and I thought this a strange discourtesy on the part of Muslims. Furthermore, a young boy cleaning the bowl we had previously drunk from seemed to be going to a great deal of trouble. With what I considered quite unnecessary ostentation, he washed it in our presence, making little noises of distaste as if our touch had rendered the bowl unclean.

Cemal shared my uneasiness. I could see that by the way he moved uncomfortably, his eyes darting from one man to the other. He bade Hikmet Bey refuse the headman's offer of a night's hospitality, saying that we had to be on our way, making the weakest excuses and fingering his revolver in pretended examination, but letting everyone know that it was loaded and that he was probably an excellent shot. I felt for my own and caught the headman regarding me thoughtfully.

A small, friendly argument broke out between Hikmet Bey and Cemal, the former protesting that his legs wouldn't carry him another inch. I tried to concentrate on something else. The sky was darkening rapidly and the beautiful jagged peaks of the distant mountains were filled with shadow. Only the trees far below us caught and held the last of the sunlight. There was a smell of newly lit dung fires and a donkey brayed quite close at hand. Hearing Cemal's high angry voice, I turned to look at him. A ring of men had surrounded us, their faces threatening our easy retreat from a situation that looked as if it might become ugly. I was reminded, more forcibly than at any time since we commenced the journey, that I was halfway up a mountain I didn't know. Dusk was falling and civilisation was a long way off. Up here in this wilderness, the laws made in Ankara didn't apply. My gun, jutting against my hip, was poor comfort. These men had guns too. There were more of them than we could overcome, and their snapping dogs looked as if, at one word, they would be willing to tear us apart.

Cemal threw them money, in payment for our tea apparently. I pulled down the sleeve of my jacket, hiding my watch, but determined to give it up if it were demanded. I reflected that heroism might be expected of me, and while I was ready to acquit myself as nobly as I knew how, I was not willing to be killed for a watch. Fortunately, the sight of the money seemed to ease the position – perhaps they were only avaricious, not killers? Yet I believe they would have killed us had we been only one or two. Men have been killed in these mountains before.

One of the men picked up the money and called us '*gavurs*'. The headman spat at our feet and said that '*gavurs*' must pay for their hospitality. Dursun Bey, stung to the quick at being likened to a Christian dog, protested that we were Muslims, but Cemal prevented any further argument taking place by herding us in front of him out of the village. Showers of stones, flung with devilish accuracy, flew all round us, and Hikmet Bey, too incensed to be as frightened as I was, turned and loosed off his gun. It spurted through the darkness, wounding a dog, I think. At any rate, a yelp of pain reached us, along with the curses of the men, although they did not return the fire. Hikmet Bey went on firing until he had exhausted his bullets and would have reloaded only we stopped him. The shouts continued after us for some time and then there was silence, which somehow was more unnerving than the shots and the noise, for at least then we had been certain that our opponents were taking no more action than to toss insults and stones after us.

We made progress as best we could, but this was not easy since the night was pitch black and the path full of loose stones and overhanging thorn trees that threatened to blind us. Our plans had been thrown out of gear by the unprepossessing village, where we had hoped to get shelter for the night. After another hour we rested.

Hikmet Bey told us that the semi-nomadic people lived on Kara-dağ during the summer months only, spending the winter in Karaman, or even Konya, where many of them worked on roads and so on. I remembered, with little satisfaction, the boast of the Ankara government that lowland and mountain Turk are one people, with the same facilities for education and advancement. I thought that this might be true to some extent for the people who lived close to towns, or on the lower slopes of mountains, but it was manifestly untrue for the semi-nomads – just as it was untrue of the Kurds and the Yürük. I wondered how many *jandarma* were brave enough to leave the near civilisation of the valleys and penetrate as far as these mountain fastnesses to serve conscription notices and the like. When I mentioned this to Hikmet Bey he replied very seriously that none did so. They would have been killed instantly.

The unfriendly villagers had called us '*gavurs*', expressing their belief that our way was different from theirs. This, of course, is largely true – we *are* different. We have had contact with Eastern and Western influences. Our ancestry is mixed. Mountain Turks more nearly resemble the Selcuks, and the Byzantine influences which held back and stultified the warrior Ottomans, made no impression on them. Even the Selcuks had changed more than they, for on their migrations across Asia and half the face of the then known world, the Selcuks had imbibed the culture and higher sophistication of the peoples with whom they had come into contact. They learned something of law and order, and the divinity surrounding kings. The Mountain Turk, on the other hand, lived little differently from his ancestors who had travelled from beyond the Aral Sea. Even his brand of Islam differed.

The Yürük and semi-nomadic tribes are predominantly Alevi Muslim, whereas the Turk of the town and city is a member of Sunni Islam. Basically, both believe there is no God but Allah and Mohammed is his Prophet, but similarity ends here. The Alevi belong to the schismatic branch of Islam who believe that their *halife*, or religious head, can only be descended from Ali, the Prophet's son-in-law. Much blood has been shed for this belief and many pretenders to the exalted position have arisen. The Alevi are fiercely opposed to all other Muslims, regarding them as infidels. The Sunni faction, on the other hand, believe that the office of *halife* should be given to the ablest man among them – thus, during the Ottoman Empire, the sultan was the one to assume the office of *halife*. The Sunni Muslims are tolerant, and not infrequently unorthodox. Their religion has been diluted by the changing times. The Alevi are partisans, and fiercely, almost fanatically, orthodox. They still practise mystical rites and shamanism. They believe in the sinlessness and infallibility of their *imams*, much as Roman Catholics believe in the infallibility of the Pope when he is pronouncing on holy doctrine. The Sunni despise them, regarding them as barbaric.

We soon started on our way again for Cemal was even more anxious than we were to reach the Yürük tents as quickly as possible. However, we still had another day's journey ahead of us, and the possibility of a night in the open. Furthermore, we had no means of knowing what sort of reception we would get from the Yürük who, also Alevi Muslims, might treat us hostilely. It was a depressing thought.

The night air was cold and I turned up the collar of my jacket. The moon was rising, giving us a little more light, but it was a deceptive, ghostly light, magnifying shadows. Once, coming out into a clearing, we saw the whole lonely landscape starkly revealed, the line of mountains on the horizon etched sharply against the sky, seeming almost on a level with ourselves. I was so tired I could have slept standing up. Dursun Bey, hampered by his blistered heels and the too sudden cold after day-long warmth, declared he could go no farther, and we sat down on a rock and he bathed his heels with the last of our water.

Hikmet Bey, testy with fatigue, wanted to go on regardless. Cemal, his voice coming out of the darkness, disembodied, made us feel the raw amateurs we were. Companionship in confined spaces, and even more when people are thrown together by circumstances, emphasises personal characteristics more sharply than any other combination of events. Tied to my companions by tiredness, inevitability, and the fear of being caught alone in the mountains in darkness, my senses were heightened. I saw the weakness of my position should the threatened argument break out, for, wearily aloof, I should be unable to take sides. I would remain the benevolent neutral, despised by both parties. At that moment, when Dursun Bey wanted to whip up a passionate denunciation of Cemal, I wanted nothing more than to sit and count the stars coming out. As it was, when appealed to for an opinion, I answered vaguely, having already recognised the unmistakable shape of Ursa Major and, being in such clear heights, longing to make use of the rare opportunity of determining whether one could really discern with the naked eye that the second star in the tail was double.

I longed for nothing better than to spend a night in the open but was afraid to do so alone. When Dursun Bey finally, and with deadly insult, worked Cemal into a rage (Cemal declaring it was a pity one of the well-aimed stones from the hostile village had not broken Dursun Bey's head), I was conscious less of the fact that presently blows would be exchanged than of the moonlight silvering the path ahead of us.

Imbued with too much imagination and too little heroism, I began to feel a stir of resentment against Hikmet Bey, whom I was now quite unfairly blaming for having landed us in this situation. Why, I demanded of myself, had he left the choice of a guide in the hands of his farm manager? The more I let this thought ride me, the more convinced I became that I was right. Intelligence had nothing to say on a moonlight night, halfway up a mountain which was a long way from law and order. Apart from everything else, we had tried Cemal's patience sorely. We had impeded his progress. We had been weaklings who developed blisters, who repeatedly wanted to sit down, who complained of aching legs and backs, who had – in short – proved ourselves incompetent amateurs. No longer subservient, he gave us the orders.

It was decided we should continue on a while longer, Cemal's idea being that soon we might reach a spot sufficiently sheltered to enable us to camp for the night. The trouble was we were ill-equipped for such an undertaking. We had no food, no water, no blankets. It was bitterly cold at such a height. Of course we should have foreseen such an emergency, or at least the possibility. We had bungled the whole thing, and had undertaken it with too little thought. The expedition, if one could dignify the adventure with such a name, had been planned on a conjunction – if. It had been built on the assumption that *if* the semi-nomadic villagers were friendly, and no one doubted they would be, they would shelter us for the night, leaving us the whole of next day to climb to the Yürük tents.

The path was so narrow that the rocks hemmed us in on either side. We flashed torches in dark places and once we had a shock when, rounding a bend, the moonlight revealed a precipice with a sheer drop to the unseen valley below us. I cowered against the rocky projection on my right, stumbling over loose, treacherous stones, and clutching the jagged edges of the rock as I stumbled. Hikmet Bey, fascinated by the nearness of death, stopped us once to fling down a tin cup into the inky depths. Several seconds later we heard it striking the bottom, or perhaps it only bounced off a ledge.

'I don't like this damned quietness,' Dursun Bey said from behind me, 'I advise everyone to have his gun ready. I have mine.'

I almost felt the ghostly prod of it in my back.

'A lot of good a gun would be here,' Cemal retorted. 'Two people couldn't pass each other on this path.'

Presently, however, the narrow defile opened out, rocks hiding the precipice. We seemed to have stopped climbing and were on a sort of plateau where the scrub grass had been cropped bare by grazing flocks. This might mean that there was a settlement near by and our spirits began to revive. We picked our way carefully but once I slipped in sheep dung and went slithering face foremost to the ground.

'Allah!' Dursun Bey cried exasperatedly, his nerves ragged with tension. 'Don't make so much *noise!*'

I picked myself up, my hands bleeding, my dignity injured, and we went on, a clump of stunted trees throwing deep shadows before us. A few thin patches of cloud obscured the brightness of the moon. The silence was immense.

Night-time fancies are irrational, corresponding to no pattern of known facts. I had the absurd idea that one of my companions, tried beyond endurance, might go mad – loose off a gun wildly, as Hikmet Bey had done earlier on, or clutch an unsuspecting throat with fingers that would relax only after all breath had been choked out of their victim. Our perseverance seemed folly and I would gladly have lain down in the place where I stood. But Cemal was inexorable. The cropped grass and the sheep droppings had excited him. Leading the way, head thrust forward, stalking like an Indian brave, he was determined not to be taken by surprise.

Hikmet Bey, alarming us all, gave a startled yelp and fell down. A horrid groan came from the place where he had fallen. My heart thumping, I flashed my torch and found him lying almost nose to nose with a startled-looking camel! He scrambled to his feet, holding his nose against the foetid breath of the camel.

Now that we were standing still, our eyes began to discern the squat shapes of tents and what might have been huts. The silence was unnerving, however, and no lights showed. We had come across the settlement unexpectedly, and Hikmet Bey spoke for all of us when he remarked in a hoarse whisper that he feared we could expect nothing good from a place where no dog barked, perched high on Karadağ like some forsaken encampment.

The dark shadows that appeared on the horizon were no more astonishing at first than events seen in a dream. I think we all remained where we were, none of us speaking, each of us perhaps convinced that what we were seeing was some personal hallucination. I remember I was afraid, uncertain whether to attempt to fly for my life or stay and shoot it out. However, the cold feel of my gun lacked its usual reassurance.

The shadows, plainly discernible now as those of men, moved forward inexorably. They were completely silent, and this was what was so terrifying. Too, the moonlight gave them added height. The camel continued to groan, and I saw Cemal take out his gun. I grasped my stick, hoping I should have time to break a few heads before my own was broken, yet still none of us moved.

Then, surprising myself as much as everyone else, although possibly it was nothing more than fear motivating me, I bounded forward: '*Selamun-aleykum, ağalar!*' I cried. 'We are your guests. We seek your hospitality for the night.'

The shadowy line of men halted, broke up into individual shapes and found voice.

'Is it a stranger?' one of them called doubtfully, and lifted a lantern above his head.

'No, no!' shouted one of his companions. 'It's a trick! Use your sticks!'

'For God's sake,' I cried exasperatedly. 'Can you not see we are strangers seeking your hospitality?'

'We are God's guests,' Dursun Bey said pompously, and in an unexpectedly loud voice.

'You are as my brothers!' Hikmet Bey declared, not daring to move however.

The lamp was held close to our faces, and I saw a large black beard behind the light.

'They are indeed travellers,' the bearded one announced, greatly surprised. 'They are indeed our brothers in God.'

I hovered on the verge of laughter. This courteous exchange of pleasantries was almost too much for me, yet all at once I felt tired, realising only then the terrible strain it had been watching them coming towards us.

We were taken to the village guest-house, but no explanation of their odd behaviour was given, nor why the entire settlement – which was bigger than we had thought – was in darkness. They seemed as embarrassed as we were at being caught in such odd circumstances, and kept clasping our hands, telling us how welcome we were.

The guest-house was one long and windowless room. A hurricane lamp was put in the centre, in danger of being overturned until one of the men had the good sense to put it on a ledge running along one wall. There was a carpet of woven *kilim* on the floor. Several tight-looking little cushions in brilliant colours were stacked against the walls. Our hosts were evidently anxious to make a fuss of us, and even went so far as to light a fire of camel dung, which would have sent us all rushing out into the fresh air again had it not been for the fear of hurting their feelings – and, perhaps, their tempers. After such an odd welcome we felt the necessity for wariness.

They brought us a bowl of soup, from which we ate noisily with wooden spoons. They brought us fried eggs, black bread and wild honey. Then they left us alone.

We speculated on our strange welcome but none of us could think of a reasonable explanation.

A little later several of them crowded into the room again, this time with straw pallets and camel-hair blankets. Dogs, vociferous now, peered in at the open door, to be dispatched with a howl into the darkness by a well-aimed kick or a sod of camel dung. They told us that in the morning we would meet the *muhtar* who, realising we must be weary, did not wish to disturb us that night. Soon they had left us, and we lay down on our straw beds too tired even to be mistrustful.

The fire died down. Outside a donkey brayed. I fell asleep fingering my gun.

6

Semi-Nomads – The Thousand and One Churches –
Lords of the Mountains – Fingers before Forks –
'For Güzel!'

WHEN I AWOKE, sunlight was filtering in through the cracks in
the ill-fitting door of the guesthouse. Cocks were crowing outside
and dogs barking. I heard a woman's voice scolding a child. I turned
over on the uncomfortable straw pallet and every muscle ached from
the previous day's unaccustomed exertion.

Cemal was already up and fully dressed and when he saw that I was
awake he threw open the door, letting in a flood of sunlight. Hikmet and
Dursun, aroused by our talking, complained of stiffness but Cemal said
he would soon put that right. Then commenced fifteen minutes of near-
torture for, starting with me, Cemal massaged the muscles of legs, thighs,
back and torso until every aching muscle had been ferreted out. His
powerful fingers dug into me relentlessly, ignoring my yelps of protest,
and by the time he had finished with me and started on Hikmet Bey, I
felt as weak as a kitten. However, after lying supine for a little while I
discovered that most of my aches had disappeared – only the deep
imprint of Cemal's fingers remained to remind me of the pummelling I
had received.

A youth brought bowls of water for us, standing by courteously
while we washed, or at least attempted to wash, for there wasn't much
water, and pouring water over our hands from a long-spouted jug.

Afterwards another youth brought tea, home-made bread (very doughy and nauseous), sheep's-milk yoghurt and wild honey. We ate in the sunlight, squatting on the dusty grass, and, despite the bread, I think food has never tasted as good.

The *muhtar* paid us a visit and we thanked him for his hospitality. He listened to us with a cool, distant curiosity, twirling his amber beads with a rapidity that made me blink. His eyes were clear and cold, like those of a bird of prey. In fact, he was very much like a bird of prey, with his lean, hungry face, the colour of leather, and his rangy body in goatskin coat. He wore a woollen cap over his greasy hair. He wore it rakishly, with an air, and he had the longest fingers I have ever seen. He enquired whether we had slept well, had we eaten enough, and to all our answers he nodded, detached from us, not over curious, merely going through the motions of host to guest.

He apologised for not having killed a sheep in our honour the previous night but the hour had been advanced, his men had had word of our arrival too late. He hoped we would forgive him. He bowed to us very formally, and we returned the salute, dropping our heads, laying our hands on our hearts. He then told us the reason for our unique welcome.

At first, when word of our approach had been given, we had been mistaken for the advance party of a raiding expedition from a village the other side of the hill. The name of this village was Maden Şehir, and he said we should give it a wide berth. The people of Maden Şehir were all thieves and bandits, they did a great deal of harm to his people. From time to time there were raids – although, he pointed out, *his* people only carried out reprisals. Being honest, God-fearing people, he said, they never sought trouble. He folded the tips of his fingers together as he said this, his expression righteous.

It appeared that a few days before our arrival there had been a dispute between the two villages, the people of Maden Şehir staking their claim to a water-hole that through long usage belonged to the *muhtar's* people. There had been a fight. Many heads had been broken, several teeth rammed down angry throats and the opposers vanquished.

The *muhtar's* tone expressed satisfaction. When a man tending goats had heard our voices in the distance, which were greatly magnified by darkness, he had hurried to the *muhtar*, convinced that we were, if not the enemy, then something totally unexpected and therefore nearly as dangerous. Strangers, the *muhtar* explained to us with a tired smile, had not been known to pass this way since before he was born. Assuming, therefore, that we were out to raid the village, the women and children and dogs had been left behind closed doors, the lights extinguished, and all the able-bodied men gathered together. We were lucky, said the *muhtar*, we had escaped harm, for his men generally shot first and asked questions afterwards. With sunlight warming our faces this point of view seemed reasonable enough.

A circle of men gathered round us, curious to hear where we had come from but, unlike the city Turk, not overly interested in where we were going. They sat round us in a semi-circle, cross-legged, offering us hand-rolled cigarettes. They looked hard and lean and tough, with bearded faces alight with interest. They displayed a harsh directness of thought that was in keeping with their weather-beaten faces and the primitive conditions under which they lived. The *muhtar* remained detached, rolling cigarettes in his incredibly long fingers and now and then permitting a smile to lighten his hooded eyes.

I asked how they lived and an old man said they bred a few sheep, whose wool and skins and the yoghurt made from their milk they sold in Karaman. They grew a little wheat which they ground by hand. The strong young men made the long journey as far as the Manavgat River to collect the bullrushes used in basket- and mat-making. Sometimes they went to the forests to cut wood, which they also sold in the town or in Konya. Such a journey might mean anything up to a week's absence from camp. They agreed that life was hard, but they added quickly that God gave them compensations. Time and distance meant little to them. There was no reason why they should ever get anywhere at a certain time; only the weather was their enemy, sometimes ruining their meagre crops or killing their sheep in snowdrifts.

We left the village early, continuing to climb upwards, escorted by a young boy called Osman. He was a real Yürük, who had been down to Karaman with a load of rushmats and was returning to the camp with a sack of rice for his family.

The distant mountain peaks were still hazed with morning and the sun was not yet too hot for comfort. Large and brazen, like a vast yellow disc, it pushed itself higher in the sky, bathing the tops of hills in saffron light although the valleys were still deep in shadow. Daylight revealed the magnificence of the country and the height we had climbed. Far, far below wound a thread of road. It looked like a vein in the barren brown flesh of the earth. There was no living thing to be seen. Once, looking back, I saw the smoke from dung fires in the village we had just left, but there was nothing else, nothing to betray the presence of the living.

The wide blue bowl of the sky curved above us, and here and there cow parsley foamed, a sudden spurt of brightness against the naked rocks. After about an hour the path became steeper, and for a time the rocks hemmed us in, claustrophobically. My leg muscles began to pull and behind me I could hear the heavy breathing of Hikmet Bey. Cemal marched ahead of us stoically. At last the rocks fell away from us, although the way continued to rise sharply. We saw sheep in the distance who, catching the echo of our voices, paused in cropping the grass to look in our direction. Dursun Bey, governed by morning skittishness, shouted, 'Baa-aa!' very loudly, and the sheep turned away disdainfully to continue cropping the grass. Only a ram with very large horns continued to stare us out. The scent of wild thyme was all around us. It covered outcropping rocks in shades of violet and mauve, its sharp perfume mingling with the dusty earth, enveloping us like a cloud.

We passed Binbirkilise – the Thousand and One Churches – a remarkable relic of Byzantium. Empty now and in ruins, the churches gape open to the sky, a memento of the ages behind us.

Picking his nose with delicate unawareness, Osman said that in winter his tribe and their flocks came down here for shelter, until the first sun of spring sent them up the mountain again to summer pastures. He knew nothing of the ruins or when they had been built, and he looked blank and uncomprehending when I mentioned the word Byzantium. Hikmet Bey said there was a legend, perhaps a prophecy, which foretold that when the whereabouts of the last church was found the world would come to an end; to date the remains of one thousand had been discovered.

I should have liked to spend some time there, wandering round the sad grey ruins, defiled now by sheep droppings and camel dung. It was like a ghost city, isolated and forgotten.

I am profoundly sentimental about ruins. They touch some responsive chord in me. The death of civilisations makes me tremble for the fate of our own, which has given so much less to posterity. Once I turned back to look at the ruins lying below us. Mist lingered about them, mingled with the searching rays of the sun, it was as if the whole place was burning in this bare mountain.

According to Osman, the Yürük sought refuge in the ruins for nearly five months of the year, from the end of October to the beginning of March, when they set out for Söğüt to celebrate the festival of spring.

'When the sun begins to warm Yürük bones, they can no longer stay in the ruins,' he explained shyly.

'But wouldn't life be easier if you stayed in the lowlands, in the villages?'

'Allah forbid! We are born to the tents, and we would die anywhere else.'

We smiled at each other a trifle sadly, conscious that each man must live according to his fate.

Later he said: 'You should see us at the spring festival! The children jump and dance, they are so excited, see? And the women cannot get things ready quickly enough. Oh, it is all rush at that time! All through the winter the tents have been repaired, new tents have been woven, cooking-pots have been relined with copper, babies have been born and the mothers want them to hurry up and grow big so that they can enjoy the festival. It is a lovely festival! We put on our embroidered clothes and everyone is happy.' His dark eyes shone, his voice broke with emotion. 'We are only happy when we move,' he added. 'When we move we are free, we are like the birds, see? The camels and the donkeys wear little bells, the children have flowers in their hair, and the men fire shots in the air.' He took an enormous breath. 'All–ah!' he said with great feeling. 'It is like being in heaven!'

The path had become so steep that he had no more breath left for talking, but now and then he squeezed my hand to show me how good he thought life was. His matted black hair fell across his eyes and his mouth trembled with happy laughter. He looked as wild and free as a bird himself.

The sun grew hotter. The stark tawny lines of the Taurus stood out against the wide arc of sky. A flight of ibis gangled overhead, their wings tinged with gold, their underbellies pink as a new-blown rose. Their graceful, skimming flight delighted our hearts while we plodded doggedly up slippery paths, clutching with amateurish eagerness at tufts of withered grass that came away in our hands. Another time we saw an eagle. It circled for a long time, then we saw it drop like a plummet or a stone from a sling, for a while disappearing from our view in the valley. After a time, however, we saw it again, climbing the air with a snake in its mouth. It flew up and up, then dropped the snake from some unfathomable height, diving after it, disappearing finally behind the rocks. I thought that the eagle was a symbol of the mountains, the isolation, the fight for survival, the cruelty.

The surrounding hills thinned out, and there was nothing but rock and scree and sun-baked earth. Far away there were sheep grazing, but I would never have known they were sheep had Osman not said so. They looked like a field of thistledown. Our feet burned in our battered shoes, the patina of newness and expensiveness now worn away. My face felt raw and burned, the two-day growth of beard an irritating excrescence. Yet despite the heat and the tiredness, I felt exalted in some way. Karadağ was my personal Everest, and I had conquered it. It meant something, but I didn't know precisely what.

We were still forced to walk in single file. We didn't talk much. Indeed, I think we were all, except Osman, voiceless with the too rapid climb. We were oppressed by the weight of the journey. We were not cast in heroic mould, yet we were fired with the ambition of heroes. The sun heeled westward, pouring a storm of light over the countryside, and the smell of thyme was everywhere.

Suddenly we came out on a wide plateau, Osman grinning delightedly at our surprised faces. The grass was unbelievably green. Sheep were grazing close to us, but startled by our sudden appearance they hurried off in another direction. There were a few camels, squatting on the earth, and a little black donkey cropping the grass beside them amicably. Lines of black hair tents showed against the horizon, and beyond them the last bit of Karadağ went up, rocky and unclimbable, to the sky.

'Here are the tents,' said Osman.

I suppose the imagination is always stirred at the sight of free men, people to whom time and earth satellites mean nothing. Here on this green plateau, with the stony heights of Karadağ looming, we had come upon a group of primitives. Their picturesque rags took one back to a braver era; so must one's ancestors have looked in the time of the Moguls. They might have been beings from another world. Indeed, their world was, in physical and spiritual terms, so far away from our own that here on Karadağ it must have been us who seemed the apparitions.

Happiness is the inheritance of the nomad, whose infinity lies about him unquestioned. Freedom is his secret. Even the limitations of the small part of the world with which he comes into contact do not harass him, for that world does not exist for him and he lives in liberty beyond it. The nomad does nothing to make the world a happier place for others. The ruins of antiquity move him not, and if it suits him he will destroy the ruins in small ways – taking a stone here, an inscribed tablet there, to hold up a sagging fence so that his animals will not roam; even to use for his own tent. But for all that, he is not destructive; he merely makes use of what is provided free. He must have discovered long ago that the meaning of life is more important than antiquity; indeed, antiquity – in the shape of ruined temples or fallen columns – by its very usefulness to him in the present, the one as a winter shelter, the other as a means of preventing his herd from straying, seems to admit of no break in continuity. The past and the present are all one to him, he is of the one and of the other equally. His freedom of the soul is on the grand scale, and this makes him unique and splendid in a world dominated by circumstances. He is built to a pattern of inevitability and accepts all things as they come to him without question, with forbearance and humour, and with the resignation that is born of simplicity.

As we passed through their close-lying goat-hair tents, the Yürük stared at us in surprise, accepting our appearance among them for the time being since Osman was with us. Their lean, magnificent dogs slunk away from us, only baring their teeth to growl low in the throat when they were at a safe distance from us.

The whole unbelievable scene was brilliant with summer and sun. The shadows of the tents were hard and clear on the ground, and a boy carving a bird on a pole was as wild and improbable as the figure he carved. The women were like bright flowers in their long striped dresses, some of them with gold coins chinking about their necks, all of them with the proud erect carriage of independence. How lovely they were in that first quick glance! Their faces had never known the restriction of the veil, their large sparkling eyes spilled over with secret laughter. They were thin and vital and superbly free. They made no effort to escape from our presence, regarding us with hands on hips, children pulling at their skirts and a monarch's easy smile on their lips.

The smoke of a fire rose up against the sky. The depth and transparent brilliancy of the day, the frolicking young ponies pounding across the emerald grass, the camel nuzzling her cream-coloured foal, all had the brittle quality of a painting on glass, idealised, ready to shatter at a too sudden movement. I was mesmerised by my first impressions, and the mesmerism is still with me. First impressions are often the last to die, and when I think of the Yürük on Karadağ, I see them behind the haze of a summer morning, with the same wildness in their eyes as that in the eyes of their animals, something farouche, nostalgic and unpredictable; something that kept us apart from the very beginning, leaving a gap in our relations with them that never closed.

The sight of them stirred my blood, and for a while obscured my judgement. Even now, looking back to that summer morning, they refuse to emerge in perspective, the perspective they *must* have had. They shift and waver, shadows on a screen, smiling their wild, shy smiles, the eternal wanderers, people outside reality.

I am a traveller only in the modern sense. I seldom go far off the beaten track, so that my journey to the Yürük tents still retains the elements of wonder and achievement. Moving among them my life was as it were suspended in another dimension. I forgot the world of time, of cities and bustle, of established law and order, and tranquillisers. I felt freer than I have ever felt in my life – yet more imprisoned because my heart searched for its reasons and my mind didn't know how to use such freedom. One has to be born to freedom to accept it. To live primitively was frighteningly easy. The daily bath was sloughed off as easily as a snake sloughs off an old skin. The bearded face was comfortable. The veneer of civilised living dropped away from us, was forgotten, had never existed – except in some life so remote it might have been lived by someone else. Sleeping and eating were no longer rituals, but moods, states of being governed strictly by fatigue and hunger. Our senses hung somewhere between enchantment and logic, touching the periphery of freedom then darting away again like a dragonfly tipsy with too much sun. We found it easy to identify ourselves with the Yürük, but impossible not to remember we were transient. We were birds of passage, ships passing in the night; with a wealth of gesture and extravagant words we wove them into our imagination. We would remember them long after they had forgotten us.

As soon as we arrived, Osman led us to the largest and most important-looking tent, which he explained was the *oba bey*'s. An *oba bey* is a nomadic chieftain, the tribe itself being called an *oba* and the chieftain's title, translated literally, meaning 'head of the tent'. I expected to be greeted by some bearded patriarch but instead a young giant welcomed us. He was tall and hungry looking but he radiated confidence, and smelt of stale sweat. When he smiled his teeth were unbelievably white and his black eyes glittered like polished stones. His personality was impressive, and it was easy to see that authority sat lightly on his shoulders. He would kill or be killed in any battle that involved his honour. He had the strongly marked face of the man who would never accept compromise; perhaps therein lay his own weakness even though, as long as he lived, it was the strength of the tribe.

He greeted us with interest, even warmth, and invited us to enter his tent. He showed much less surprise at our appearance among his people than we had expected. With kingly gesture, and a flashing of those unbelievable teeth, he preceded us into the murky depths of the tent where, for a moment or two, the combined fumes of camel dung and humanity almost stifled me.

Osman, who had not come in with us, had also neglected to inform us on certain points of etiquette, inflexible within the tribe so we afterwards learned. I suppose Osman took these things for granted, perhaps he even expected that in the outside world from where we came these exquisite courtesies were also practised. At any rate, we were asked to be seated. Hikmet Bey, who was the oldest among us, took his place on a pile of cushions close to the fire, believing, as we did, that this important place was reserved for guests. This, at least, was the host–guest relationship of the villages on the plains. I took a seat near the tent-flap, hoping in this way to get enough fresh air to minimise the heavy smell of the tent. Dursun Bey and Cemal sat near me. There were a few other men in the tent whom I took to be relatives of the *oba bey*. Each one of them bade us welcome, rising to his feet, bowing to us with his hand on his breast and murmuring: '*Selamun-Aleykum*'; shooting up from our places we returned the compliment, touching foreheads and breasts in salutation. It was a long time since I had sat cross-legged but I found the posture surprisingly comfortable, and not without dignity.

All this time the *oba bey* had remained standing, and I began to feel embarrassed, wondering if this was a sign we were unwelcome. Hikmet Bey begged him to be seated but he refused, smilingly. Conversation, which could scarcely be said to have ever flourished, now died down to a few spasmodic questions and answers. It was only rescued from total extinction by an old man who ever since our entrance had been feeding the fire with dung. He muttered that the *oba bey* couldn't sit down because Hikmet Bey had already occupied his seat! This information sent a scarlet-faced Hikmet Bey rocketing from his place, scattering cushions and camel saddles, apologising and bowing wildly in the direction of the impassive *oba bey*, who had more than enough dignity to spare.

The *oba bey*, able to sit down at last, restored our confidence by offering hand-rolled cigarettes and calling for tea. We learned that seating is strictly controlled, and has, in fact, a language of its own. The master's seat is known as 'the place of the warrior', and is inviolate. As long as Hikmet Bey remained in this place the *oba bey* had to stand, for this was a sign of his friendly intentions towards us. Had he sat elsewhere the other men would have realised, without a word being said, that he was ill disposed to have us among his tribe. He would have fed us and enter-tained us but all this would have been meaningless, and the moment we had departed from his tent his enmity would have been given verbal, perhaps concrete expression. To illustrate his point further, he told us that his grandfather, when he was dying, had quitted life in the 'place of the women' rather than remain in the 'place of the warrior' in the presence of his lifelong enemy, who had entered the tent merely to heap this last insult on a dying man. We were impressed by such strength of character.

Every corner of a tent has its own language. The 'place of the warrior' is, of course, the most important. In the *oba bey*'s tent it was a silver-chased camel saddle heaped with embroidered cushions. A bearskin rug, with more cushions, was for guests. Placed along the 'walls' of the tent were more cushions and these were where neighbours gathered. The 'place of the women' was inconspicuous behind the fire.

More people kept coming in while we were there, and this necessitated interrupting one's conversation to stand up and return the salute murmured in one's direction. After a time, we seemed to be more often up than down. The courtesy was exquisite, if laboured. The younger men spoke only when the ponderous formalities of the *oba bey* and the older men were done with.

Tobacco tins were thrown into the centre of the bearskin rug, an invitation for us to help ourselves. The talk was quick and earnest. Questions flew off their tongues like quicksilver, but always questions of a general nature. They never asked us where we were going after we left them, accepting the fact that we might well spend the rest of our lives with them. They were full of stories of old times. They talked because they liked talk, and because they had something of interest to say. Each one was a storyteller in his own way, with variations of style and subject. None of them envied us, neither did they pity us. We were all members of one vast brotherhood, where the worth of a man was not judged by his political affiliations.

We made it clear that we would like to spend a short time among them, and the *oba bey* said he would have a tent erected for us. This, he assured us, would be no trouble at all. We were welcome to everything he had. It was impossible not to believe him. He was the soul of honour, an aristocrat of the nomads. Indeed, all the Yürük men impressed me with their easy acceptance of life and their almost perfect communal living. They had their differences, obviously, but they were less inclined to sudden violence than the men of the cities, and their nervous systems were superb. Their simplicity was disarming. They had no need of innuendo or prevarication; they spoke their minds without dissembling.

Towards early evening a tray of *pilav* was brought in and a whole roasted lamb. We were invited outside the tent where a boy poured water over our hands, and we went through the symbolic gestures of washing ourselves. The air was deliciously cool and the level light of evening spread out between the peaks of distant mountains. Smoke rose from every tent, and the whole scene was pastoral and infinitely tender. I breathed in the good clean air and felt my heart lift within me.

Inside the tent we discovered the difficulties of eating sitting cross-legged on cushions. Only Cemal, who had perhaps had more experience than we, seemed unconcerned. Every man helped himself with his fists and a wad of black bread. We scooped the rice in our fingers, the back of the right hand thrust into the *pilav*, staking a claim for ourselves. The lamb was torn to pieces by ruthless fingers, and our hosts, noting that their guests were being bashful, courteously dropped the best bits on our personal mound of rice. I had never realised before how difficult it is to eat without implements. No matter how sure we were that we had scooped up the rice without danger of losing it before it reached our mouths, still each of us found only a crumb or two clinging to our greasy fingers. The floor was soon spattered with rice. The *oba bey*, noticing our difficulties, called for wooden spoons, and wielding these we were filled with shame, but at the same time with food, and this seemed to us to be the more important.

We retired once more to have warm water poured over our hands, but mine still felt greasy. A huge pot of sheep's-milk yoghurt was brought in, and we all dipped our spoons into the same pot, apologising with strained courtesy when two of us tried to stake a claim in the same place. Eating was the only time the Yürük showed their wolflike instincts. Filled with food, I loosened the top button of my trousers and belched louder than anyone else – thus shaking my belief that man is a civilised animal. Nobody took the slightest notice, except Hikmet Bey, who raised his eyebrows, and Dursun Bey, who tut-tutted with embarrassment.

After our meal we sat outside in the gathering dusk, the *oba bey* rolling cigarettes at an incredible speed and passing them to us. I do not smoke and this obviously worried him, and he tried to press melon seeds on me instead, assuring me that these were good for the digestion. To please him, I chewed a few, but spat them out when nobody was looking.

Dusk was a time of sociability. The women of the family gathered round us, smiling, excited, with the charming ease of intercourse of the free. They were a handsome crowd, with lean figures and upright carriage. Their faces were brown with sun and wind, their eyes fiercely intelligent; only their hands were toilworn.

The oldest of them, the *oba bey*'s mother, bade us welcome in the name of the Yürük women. She wore a faded red blouse, fastened across the breast with a pin. Two of her grandchildren clung to her voluminous black skirt, their uncombed hair falling across their eyes, the youngest child sucking her thumb and peering at us shyly. The woman disengaged her skirt from their fingers and sat down opposite us. She was perhaps a little over fifty, but wind and rain had beaten all traces of youth from her face; only her fine dark eyes were alert and vivacious. She told us she had never been farther than Binbirkilise in her life. She had never seen a village, she knew only the life of the tents and was content that this should be so. She talked fluently, with expressive gestures. She had borne eighteen children, all of whom were alive. In her youth she had been the best weaver of tents in the whole camp; nowadays, her daughter-in-law held that honour.

In answer to a question about the tents, she said: 'Yürük women build the tents. Like the birds we build our own nests. We weave, and then we build.'

'But don't the men build?' I asked.

'We build,' she replied patiently.

The tents were simply constructed. There was a tall centre pole, always beautifully carved by one of the men with the figures of birds or animals, which was used to hang rifles on and other masculine paraphernalia that might be needed in a hurry. There were four poles on each of the two longest sides of the tent, and two poles along each remaining side. The tent, of goat or camel hair, was laid across the poles and bound securely at the bottom edges. A hole was left in the roof for smoke to escape through, but the hole was so small that the tents were always filled with smoke. A sort of channel was dug all round the tent so that water could run away easily; this work was done by the women too.

The women worked as hard as the men – perhaps harder, when one remembered that in addition they had to bear children. But no thought of the hardness of their lives crossed their minds; you could see that as they spoke. They had no time for softness. This is my life, their gestures seemed to say, and it's a good one, their merry eyes replied. They were not deferential to their men, meeting them on equal terms. They showed fortitude and patience, and so rare was it for them to protest, that the one woman among them who did has left an indelible memory behind her. They told me the story, sitting there in front of the *oba bey*'s tent, with the first stars burning in the east and the moon coming up over the horizon.

Her name was Güzel (Lovely), and she was the daughter of the *oba bey* of a Yürük tribe beyond Karadağ. She was as beautiful as her name and everybody spoiled her. When she was a little girl, her father had refused to let her do any rough work with her mother or sisters, and all day long she sat and dreamed in the sun and grew lovelier and lovelier. She had never woven a tent in her life, nor embroidered a cushion, nor made a rug, nor herded sheep on the mountain. She did nothing but look beautiful, and the whole tribe loved her. Her name has been perpetuated in song; it is still the battle-cry of Yürük warriors.

However, she was as proud as she was beautiful, and wilful too, and as she grew older she did only what pleased her – but as this was mostly sitting in the sun dreaming, that was nothing new. She fell in love with a young man of her tribe – as handsome as she was beautiful, as daring as she was gay. But never a word of love passed between them; he was too ashamed to ask the *oba bey* for the hand of his beautiful daughter, and she was too proud to plead with her father. Yet their eyes talked for them. They burned with love; their love consumed them so that they could neither eat nor sleep and were dumb in each other's presence.

Her father betrothed her to the *oba bey* of Karadağ, a man nearly thirty years older than herself. Still the young man did not speak, and now, a betrothed girl, she could not. They were lost to each other. Death could not have been more irrevocable than betrothal, for betrothal was a sacred promise and a matter of her father's pride. Were she to refuse to marry, she would start a blood feud between the tribes which would last for centuries, maybe for ever. For the Yürük only death can avenge broken pride. The *oba bey* of Karadağ would have to kill a male relation of Güzel's, and then her tribe would have to kill one of his. So it would have continued, time making no difference. Indeed, time *had* made no difference, and every so often – perhaps once in each generation – blood was still spilled for Güzel.

At last the day came for her to depart across the mountains to her new home. On Karadağ there was rejoicing and merriment. The *oba bey*'s tent had been decorated. There were new bearskin rugs, new cushions and a silver-decorated saddle for the bride. His sons and their wives and children wore their best embroidered clothes. The gift of a cream camel had been prepared for Güzel and it too was decorated, and it wore a blue bead on its forehead, not only to protect it from the Evil Eye but to protect Güzel also.

The pale proud Güzel captivated her husband, yet from the very first day she was intractable, refusing to carry out any of the jobs done by the women. She refused to soil her hands and would fly into a blazing rage that even a beating wouldn't quench. The people on Karadağ were angry with their *oba bey* for putting up with her. His authority lessened and his sons spoke openly of deposing him. How could they respect a leader who was so soft with his wife? Still he would not divorce Güzel and send her back to her own tribe, no matter how far she tried his patience. As for Güzel, she grew more beautiful than ever, and more wilful.

Time passed and word of her disobedience reached her own tribe. Her brothers set out for Karadağ to whiplash her for breaking their honour, but she spat in their faces and, with a tent-pole in her hands, dared them to come near her. In return, her husband beat her for spitting in a guest's face. In the meantime, the young Yürük she had loved so long resolved to avenge her humiliation. Gathering a party of men, he set out to attack the people of Karadağ. Güzel, hearing of their arrival, met them at the head of the narrow pass where yesterday we had smelled the wild thyme. He and she did not speak to each other. They only looked and looked, and still beset by foolish pride she tossed her head at him and ran back to warn her husband. This much, and no more, did honour demand.

While the men fought outside, Güzel, in her tent, twined gold coins in her hair and about her breasts; then, emerging from the tent, she watched the battle. The women had joined in to help their men, but Güzel leaned against the tent, encouraging her lover by her silence and her stance. Exchanging one long burning look of love with her, the young man drew his sword, shouted 'For Güzel!' and mortally wounded the *oba bey*'s eldest son. He himself was wounded soon after and Güzel, beside herself now with emotion, dashed into battle on his side, taunting the men of her husband's tribe who tried to stop her, insulting the women who sought to tear her hair out. Her lover swayed on his horse from loss of blood, falling to the ground. Güzel tended him, tearing off strips from her clothing to stanch his wounds, but he died even while they were pulling her away from him.

Proud and defiant to the last, she cried out to the watching women: 'They are not men who spring from your loins for you have no men to seed men!'

Shamed by this slur, the women flung themselves on her, tearing the clothes from her body. Kicking and struggling, shouting insults, she was brought before the *oba bey*, and the women demanded her death. But the *oba bey* declared that death was too good for her. Death was too swift and easy. He would whip her instead.

The women were put outside the tent and Güzel and the *oba bey* were left alone. Proudly she faced him, proudly she bit her teeth into her lips to prevent herself from crying out as the whip cut through her tender skin. Those waiting outside the tent heard never a sound from her, only the noise of the whip tearing the air with violence, lacerating her body, and the tears of the *oba bey* as he besought her to beg for forgiveness so that he could stop beating her. But not a word passed the lips of the proud Güzel, and the beating ceased at last only because the *oba bey* had no more strength left in his arms. Later she was thrust out into the darkness, an outcast from the tribe whose pride she had outraged. They let her take the camel she had been given as a wedding gift. They gave her a loaf of bread and a jug of water. They gave her a camel-hair cloak to cover her nakedness, and then with stones and curses they drove her out of their midst.

For many more years she lived at the edge of their camp, still proud, still wild, still beautiful. After a while, pitying her, they gave her the materials to erect a tent, but she sat in the midst of the things they gave her and taunted the men, who, unable to stoop to such menial work as erecting a tent, slunk away from her insults. Her brothers came to take her back to her old home but she sent them away again. She would die on Karadağ, she said.

Through the years the blood feud was reopened, the men of both sides taking as their battle-cry: 'For Güzel!' thus perpetuating her and her lover for ever, while she sat aloof on the spur of the hill, indifferent that it was in her name they killed each other.

The small children of the tribe brought her the leavings of their elders and these she accepted with royal condescension, occasionally upturning a pot of yoghurt on a child's head if it was too sour for her liking. She was impervious to wind and rain, sleeping out in all weathers, never losing her fragile beauty, nor her devilish pride. As long as she lived she was a reminder to the tribe of the shame she had brought on them.

The *oba bey* died, and the new *oba bey* sought to drive her from the mountain, but it was said she put a spell on him, bewitching him in a night so that he pined away and died within a week. This made her greatly feared, and many people made a long detour rather than pass the spot where she sat continually. Winter and summer she remained at the top of the mountain. The people said the devils fed her and the vultures came to shelter her from the cold at night with their wings. She tamed a raven to eat scraps from her hand, and he stayed with her, perched on her gaunt shoulder, croaking defiance at all who came near them. He was as gaunt as she was.

She lived to a ripe old age, the raven – or another raven perhaps – always with her. The men who had been children when she was a woman grew old and died, but Güzel lived on, impervious to time and the elements. Then one morning she disappeared, and although they searched for her everywhere they never found her. Had she gone some-where else to die? Nobody ever knew. Her secret remains her own.

The woman who told the story was lucid and calm, but one felt the remnants of an old shame. Yet beauty is rare, and when they speak of Güzel there is an edge of sadness to their voices, a fleeting regret. Time is softening them. One day she might even become a heroine. Meanwhile, raiding parties still set out with her name on their lips.

Her story made a vivid impression on the mind. Looking at the great round moon silvering the countryside, I could understand why the people were reluctant at night to pass the spur of rock where she is said to have lived. It juts out darkly in the distance, and even the not so very imaginative might be forgiven if they thought they saw her move against the darkness. They say a raven still lives there.

7

The Man of the Mountains – Yürük Wedding –
Riding Bareback – The Mad Shepherd –
Folk Tales – The Sword Dance

MAHMUD was the oldest Yürük on Karadağ. Some said he was over one hundred years old, others said he was about a hundred. He settled all disputes when the *oba bey* was absent from the camp, and because of his great age he was felt to have garnered all the wisdom of the ages.

He was a gentle old man, who had outlived several wives, and he invited us to his tent. We admired the variety of sporting guns hanging from the centre pole, and a small great-grandson told us proudly that the old man could still shoot better than many of the younger men. This pleased Mahmud, who began to tell us stories of his fame as a hunter.

'I am a man of the mountains,' he said. 'I live by my gun.' He grinned at me toothlessly. 'Eh!' he said. 'I can still run with the best of them!'

He fondled the guns lovingly, taking an old bit of rag out of his pocket to polish the butts. He said that sometimes brigands, fleeing from the *jandarma*, raided the camp; sometimes army deserters; even occasionally, from another village, young men came to steal a Yürük girl. He spoke of his own young days and the excitement of a raid.

'But we never went to kill,' he said. 'Not like the youth of today. We went for the sport, and sometimes we were lucky and we carried away a fine young girl for ourselves. There's one of them still here. She's nearly as old as I am now, but she was a lovely girl.'

He spoke of a wedding we had missed by about a week. He put the gun he had been polishing back on the pole with the others, his intelligent old eyes lighting with mischief as he spoke of weddings. Sometimes, he told us, a Yürük wedding is in preparation for years, from the time the affianced couple are children. As the time for the marriage ceremony draws near, sugar and little coloured candles are sent out to neighbouring tribes, the one symbolising the sweetness of love and the other the lightness of a happy heart. The wedding is performed by the *oba bey*. All the camp takes part in the celebrations. For weeks, maybe months, the women have been embroidering new clothes. The camels are decorated with beads and ribbons. Wrestling matches are arranged between the young men of visiting tribes. Musicians tune up, and the dancing and the merriment go on for two whole days. During this time vast quantities of food and drink are consumed, and as the Yürük are, generally, so poor, it isn't any wonder they spend so many years saving up for a daughter's wedding. The green, white and red Yürük flag is flown from the bridal tent, and when the marriage has been consummated the bridegroom fires a shot into the air. This is a signal for every man to let loose his own gun and, naturally, accidents are prone to happen. Mahmud told us with a chuckle that he remembered a young Yürük who had had his penis shot off. He added that, nowadays, people are more careful; the young men haven't any spirit left, he said, and heaved a great sigh for the tempestuous days of his youth.

Instructing a small boy to attend to the fire, and seating himself in the 'place of the warrior', he told us of the wedding we had been too late for. It had been the wedding of one of his grandsons, and because the father was dead, Mahmud had played a star role.

'But I tell you,' he said, 'it's no joke at my age being father-in-law to an upcoming young bride!'

He spat into the fire reflectively, extracting pleasure from the fact that he had an audience.

At last he said: 'Eh, dear me! These women of ours! Why, they break a water jar on your head if you don't give them everything they want! Anyway, that morning I dressed myself up in the clothes I wore at my own wedding eighty years ago, and when my granddaughters saw me they all laughed at me, and said they'd never seen anything so funny in their lives.

'The smell of the camphor sticks nearly killed me, and for all that the moths had got into the clothes and had eaten a long line down the back of the coat – so what did the women of the tent do but embroider the place with roses! There were roses of every colour, for they ran out of embroidery silk halfway through, but when they'd finished the coat was as good as new and I felt like a bridegroom myself!' Here he gave us a sly, meaningful look, and fingered his groin so that we wouldn't be able to mistake his meaning. 'Well,' he continued, 'I went to fetch the bride. When I reached her tent I shouted in at her: "Maiden, are you ready?" but nobody answered me, and there wasn't a sound from inside the tent. I shouted for her a second time, and her mother pulled back the flap of the tent and asked me what money I was willing to give for the maiden. "Where would I get money, old woman?" I said, for it's not right the way these women give themselves airs at a wedding. "No money, no maiden," said the woman and let fall the flap in front of my very nose. Well, I tell you, I chattered with rage – pretending she didn't care whether she married the girl off or not, when everyone knew she was a plain lump that wouldn't be to everyone's fancy – and in any case, I tell you, I don't know what came over my grandson, and I think they must have given him a philtre! Well, I fumed, but it was no good. They wouldn't let the girl out. "Here," I said in the end, "take this for her," and I pushed some money in under the flap of the tent; but in a minute she was back facing me again, and the look of rage on her face was enough to make a man tremble. "Shame on you, you old goat!" she taunted me. "Am I expected to give away a fine girl for as little as that?' Well, I gave and I gave. I tell you, I thought I'd never be finished counting out the money to her. She was a hard one, that one. I think her mother must have been a camel. In the end, when she saw I hadn't another *kuruş* to give her, she let the girl out. The other women mounted her on a fine horse, all groomed and decorated, and a fine stepping horse it was too. I led the horse, with the girl sitting up there like a queen, and when we came near to the bridegroom's tent, what happened but *his* men stopped me too to demand more money. Well, I tell you, and me one of the family! "Do you think I'm made of money?" I asked, but it was no use. They wouldn't let us pass and I had to bring more money out of my sock where I'd hidden it from the girl's mother. I had to give something to every one of them and never has a wedding cost me as much before.

'I led the girl and the horse a bit forward, and the flute-players and the men with the drums gathered behind us, and the horse was afraid and began to prance up and down. Well, I held on to it as best I could and we got to the wedding tent at last. "Come down, my daughter," I said to the girl, but she never moved. "Are you dead, girl?" I shouted, losing patience with her. "Have you lost the use of your tongue as well as your legs?" But still never a word did she say, or a move did she make. All the people began to laugh at me, and in a temper, I said, "What do you want now, girl?" and at that she opened her big mouth and said, "The wedding gifts." Well, we had to wait while the young boys brought up the goat and the ass and the six young ewes for her, and then she got down off her horse. Still she wasn't pleased. The ass was lame, she said. The goat wouldn't give milk. The ewes were so old they were only fit for *pilav*. So we had to give her six more of the best and a young camel as well. Only then would she go in to the bridegroom, mind you! I tell you, it's not easy to act as a father-in-law these days!'

He had spoken with humour and vivacity, his hands gesticulating, his eyes full of laughter, yet I think he spoke more to himself than to us, using us only as a means of releasing his memories. When he had finished what he wanted to say, he looked tired and old, weary of our company now that he had nothing more to tell us. I suppose nowadays life gave him few excitements, and few opportunities of boasting. As soon as we could we bade him good-night, but he had become querulous, uncertain who we were, and what we were doing in his tent. We went outside into the cool night air.

We were tired too. The day had been long. Looking back, it seemed as if it had lasted forever, and I longed for sleep. Two young men led us to our tent, which had been strewn with fresh straw, over which hand-made carpets had been laid. Other carpets lined the 'walls' of the tent and on the floor were a pile of cushions and a few camel-hair rugs to cover us.

The silence was ringing in my ears, although now and then it was broken by the distant crying of a jackal. At least I think it was a jackal. At any rate, it was thin and inhuman and mysterious. Up there on Karadağ, it might have been anything. By the light of my torch I saw that it was not yet eleven o'clock. In Ankara, theatregoers were beginning to crowd the nightclubs; in Istanbul, people were dining out under coloured lights in casinos beside the Bosphorus. I was so tired I could have slept for ever. Cemal turned over on his side with a grunt, flinging out a hand that, even in sleep, remembered to feel for his gun. It was like being alone on the rim of the world, and I pulled the rug over my shoulders, conscious of chill.

During the days, Osman made himself our guide. All the people seemed friendly, inviting us to their tents to drink thin, green tea or to sample a bowl of freshly made yoghurt. The dark-eyed children were enchanting, following us barefoot and wide-eyed, viewing the chocolate we gave them with gravest suspicion, never with cupidity. The old men and old women were impressive for their serenity, their slow thoughtful stare, and the manner they had of deliberating before replying to a question. They were not eager to hear of life outside their tents, and when Hikmet Bey spoke of water that came from taps, in houses where people lived all their lives, they sighed commiseratingly, and one old woman said: 'Ah, God help them, everyone has their own troubles.'

We met Gül, who was said to be ninety and who had been kidnapped by a Yürük warrior when she was only thirteen. For over three-quarters of a century she had lived on Karadağ and when we questioned her she could remember nothing of her village or her parents. She had several Yürük sons, many grandchildren and great-grandchildren, and she had the reputation of still being the best bread-maker among the women. She was making *sebit* when we met her, thin wafers of crisp golden bread that melted in the mouth, and while Osman was telling us of the fame of her beauty as a young girl, she giggled gently, pleased with the attention she was receiving. Nowadays, she spent her time breadmaking and fetching water from the spring well, three miles away across rough stony country. She looked surprised when we said it must be a hard life at her age.

The life of insecurity is the nomad's achievement. Stability has no meaning for him. It is a mode of expression, a feeling he rejects instinctively, not believing in it. He is too realistic to believe in stability. Just as time does not govern him, neither does conformity. He conforms to tribal customs it is true, but only in so far as his own nature permits. He is, in fact, the only free man left in the world.

On Karadağ, it was noticeable that the people did what pleased them not what seemed most expedient. Women were to be seen weaving goat- or camel-hair rugs, baking, making yoghurt, embroidering, chattering animatedly, unconcerned with any more serious business than that which occupied them for the moment. Children were sent off to the forest to gather the wild honey of the tree bees. They would be gone a whole day, through snake-infested country, barefoot, ragged, armed with stout sticks. From the time they were able to walk they were taught to make themselves useful. Young girls patted mounds of camel dung into palm-sized rounds, building them to dry in the sun, balancing them with dexterity so that the air could circulate freely.

The men didn't seem to do much, especially about the camp, which seemed exclusively the women's domain. The few fields of corn and wheat they tended in desultory fashion when driven to activity by the women. Some of them set off in parties to cut timber in the forests. They would be absent from camp for days, maybe weeks, and when they returned they would saw the wood into manageable sizes to sell in Karaman, or even farther afield. With the money they would buy cotton, candles, rice and sugar, toiling once more up Karadağ. Distances meant little, and Yürük women were accustomed to being without their husbands for weeks at a time.

During our second day in camp a party of men and dogs went rabbiting. Another party was going to shoot birds and Dursun Bey and I accompanied them, mounted on mettlesome young horses that had never known a saddle. I had never ridden bareback before, so I was more put out than the horse. She was a temperamental mount, with a soft mouth and a flowing tail that streamed out behind her like the drapery on Greek statues. She resented my weight, and made several efforts to throw me off. I only learned afterwards she had never been ridden before. Her method at first was to trot sedately, lulling me into inattention. Suddenly she would kick up her back legs, nearly sending me flying across her head, then whinnying with anger when I refused to be unseated. My triumph had nothing to do with good horsemanship, however. It was achieved entirely by fear and consequent reflex action, causing me to grip my knees tight against her bony sides while hanging on to the halter for dear life. Disliking the painful pressure of my knees, she next tossed her head sharply and bounced me high in the air, the noise made by my already bruised bottom coming once more in contact with her tough back ringing out like a pistol-shot. Osman, who rode beside me, was far too polite to give way to the merriment with which he struggled, and I envied him his quiet horse and his superb seat. He and his horse might have been part of each other.

Until tugging (but I was afraid to ruin the delicate mouth) and hard swearing had reduced the mare to temporary subjugation, I had little time to be aware of scenery or pay attention to Dursun Bey's conversation. Once, however, we drew rein, the mare breathing noisily, lathered in perspiration from her efforts, and I talked to her, stroking her mane, thinking to quieten her. She was not intractable, just nervous, hating this curtailment of her freedom. She bucked again, taking me by surprise, and I clung on with difficulty. I wished we were on a flat road, where I could have let her have her head, riding her to exhaustion and meekness.

Despite my preoccupation with her, I felt like a king. There is something to be said about being astride a horse that brings out noble instincts in man. Shading my eyes with my hand, I looked out across the lonely mountainside, the mare temporarily distracted by the grass at her feet, which she grazed daintily, forgetting me. On every side the rocky slopes fell away. Westward, the rocks declining, we could see exposed the tops of dark foliage gathered in a valley that was full of noonday shadow, lying in drifts of blue and purple in the hollows. To the east the land shelved downwards in a composed pattern of green fields, where a few sheep grazed. Brilliant light scintillated along the grey-green scrub. Daisies with bright yellow hearts lay bruised beneath the feet of the horses. Beside a thin stream, young poplars grew, their flat gold leaves fluttering gently. Above us, piled-up rocks mounted against the sky.

Far away, an infinity away, I think, an empty road wound through the barren land. Sharp with light, the distant mountains etched darkly against the horizon, the scene surprised me with its more than loneliness, its hint of prehistoric sadness. It was savage land, coarse-grained and inhospitable, yet I would have liked to ride on for ever, beyond the rim of the distant mountains, into some mythical land whence there would be no return.

Here, on this sun-soaked ridge, the day stood still in a safe hour, and looking back along the way we had come I was caught in a nostalgia I could not understand. For an insane moment I felt halted in a no man's land somewhere between today and tomorrow, looking back to a world that held no sanctuary for me, since the only sanctuary was forgetfulness, perhaps annihilation. The strength of this nihilism surprised me, and I wondered if I might be suffering from sunstroke, for to imagine that the spirit might be straining towards some greater truth was too embarrassing a thought to countenance.

Up here the silence was as profound as eternity, the earth itself had settled into timeless tranquillity. Was my melancholy generated by the rarefied air? I could never live this moment again in precisely the same way; even as I speculated on the cause of my sadness, feeling the soft trembling movements of the mare under me, the moment was speeding away from me, ephemeral, already fading in the swirling mists of other moments. I felt as if I had communed with God.

In all that long morning of sunshine we saw no signs of habitation – were we only phantoms in a world that no longer existed? – save a shepherd's hut from which a dog ran out to snap at the heels of the horses. We reined in to salute the shepherd who came out to greet us. He was a tall handsome youth, with a bright cloth wound round his head and goat-hair trousers fastened at the waist with string. His shirt was in tatters, opened down the front, exposing his brown chest and hollow ribs. He was nursing a sick lamb, and in his dark eyes wandered a gentle madness and a hint of the faraway places we knew nothing about. He spoke to us in soft tones, a man who spent his life in the open, disdaining even the rough amenities of camp life. Osman whispered that he was a hermit. He had no woman, no child, nothing but his dog and the sheep he tended for others, and now and then a sick lamb to nurse, to waken the tenderness he was unable to give to human loved ones.

'He's mad,' Dursun Bey said, his horse shying away.

But perhaps it was less madness than inattentiveness that shone in his eyes. Horses and men crowded him in against the sagging door of his hut, and once he put his hand over his eyes in a pathetic gesture of distaste against our noisy exuberance.

'He was born in the tents,' Osman explained. 'His mother was a Wise Woman. She was able to cure every disease on earth, but she couldn't cure his father who was crushed under a camel in a terrible camel fight down in Karaman. Neither could she cure herself, and when she died he came to live here. That's nearly twenty years ago.'

We jogged on again, leaving the shepherd staring after us with those piercingly beautiful eyes that seemed to see right through us. I was in half a mood to dismount and go back to him, but as if reading my thoughts he went back into the hut, closing the door behind him.

'Tell me about him,' I said to Osman.

'There's nothing to tell. He's mad. They say he was touched by the jinn. He dances alone in the moonlight, his dog's howling making music for him. One night last winter he frightened my sister nearly to death. She was coming with water from the well just beyond this place. From a long way off she could see him, throwing up his hands, prancing naked in the moonlight, and the snow thick on the ground, and the dog leaping beside him, keening as if there had been a death. My sister lay hidden until he stopped dancing and had gone inside again, and then she crept past his hut, praying he wouldn't come out again. But the dog heard her and flew at her throat, and the baby she was carrying in her belly fell at her feet with the fear she was in.'

I looked at him, suspecting him of lying, but the men riding behind us, who had overheard the conversation, assured me it was so; they remembered Osman's sister and the madman.

'Well, what happened then?' I asked, and Osman looked puzzled.

'Why, nothing more,' he said. 'She came home with the baby and got a good beating from her husband who thought she had been with another man.'

'That's so,' put in one of the men behind. 'I remember it well.'

Their simplicity and their cruelty defeated me. At no point did our minds meet.

We halted to eat *sebit*, goat's cheese and raw onion, and rarely has a meal tasted so good as on that cool mountain day, with the smell of horses and men and wild thyme. Good temper is a Yürük characteristic. Even when they beat their wives or their children, it is generally on the principle that chastisement guards purity. But of true kindliness they seemed to know nothing. The sufferings of their fellows left them curiously detached, and they bore their own with heroic stoicism. A strange characteristic for a mountain people, they had no respect for nature, uprooting young trees without a thought and cursing the blazing sun that burned them black as negroes.

When we rode on again, an eagle followed us, wheeling low over our heads. His wing-span was enormous, and with the light gilding his feathers he looked like some magnificent image fashioned in bronze. The men said there were two of them and that they lived on the top of Karadağ. Once, a Yürük youth climbed to their eyrie to steal one of their young. The parents had beaten him to the ground with their great wings and had then pecked out his eyes. Managing to save himself, he had staggered back to the Yürük camp, his face streaming with blood and his eyes hanging out on his cheeks as if on stalks.

We shot our first bird soon after we had seen the eagle. A rifle cracked and a fine partridge fell at our feet. The shot had disturbed the nesting birds, and soon there were many of them beating the air, their cries low and creaking. They flew blindly in the path of the guns, easy victims. In all, eighteen birds were gathered by the men, the legs tied together and the glossy heads hanging limply. I had not fired a shot, not out of compunction for the nesting birds, but because, familiar as I am with a revolver, I was uncertain of the aged shotgun they had given me. Added to that, the cavorting mare and the men milling backwards and forwards filled me with dread. I had no wish to behead a Yürük.

We rode back in the late afternoon, the dead birds swinging from the sides of the horses. To the east the sky was intensely, coldly blue but in the west it burned like gold. A hen harrier, the first I had ever seen, came scudding downwind, its white breast brilliant in the level light. I had a glimpse of its cruel yellow beak and the exquisite tracery of blood-red veining on its bluish feathers before it swooped down behind a rock, perhaps after a snake.

We passed the shepherd's hut, calling out a welcome, but his door was closed and there was no sign of him or his dog. We left a partridge for him, one of the men calling to him loudly that there was a partridge at his door and to make sure the dog didn't get it. There was no answer from the hut, yet we all felt he was inside, listening to us in the darkness, holding up a hand to keep the dog from barking. Everywhere was as still as the grave. One felt it must be lonely there at night.

The upward climb to the camp was stiff and the little mare I rode was too tired to display any tantrums. I patted her neck and promised her a handful of sugar at the end of the journey. It was dusk when we reached the camp and when I dismounted my legs felt as heavy as iron clamps. Bidding Osman hold the little mare, I hobbled to our tent to bring her some sugar, which she refused to eat until I had thrown it on the ground.

Later I sat outside the tent with a group of old men who smoked tranquilly and told tales of their youth. The sun looked like a great orange. Distant hills were humped grotesquely against a flaming background, where the brilliant colours of a summer sunset flared in splendour.

Evening is veiled in romance in a Yürük camp, at least for the traveller who has nothing more onerous to do than sit and watch. Wisps of dung smoke curled lazily against the sky. The smell of cooking meat was wafted in tantalising drifts, making my mouth water. The voices of young children were muted in the spell of evening and inside dark tents babies were being sung to sleep. This was the witching hour between sunset and nightfall, and in the east Venus glittered. Lamps were not yet lit, and in the half-darkness the women flitted to and fro like grey shadows, mysterious, inaccessible, the harbingers of life and death. The mournful eyes of a camel stared at me across a tent, his groans deep with hatred and longing; impossible to believe that camels groan merely because they like to.

The old men were still swapping reminiscences for the benefit of the stranger who wasn't listening, their voices a quiet muttering in the background of his thoughts. And always, it seemed to me – although since I heard only snatches perhaps I was wrong – they talked of times past, of youth and beauty and valour. Only in their memories did they live again. The women of their youth were more beautiful than any now living. The men were braver. Even the weather was different. In their recollections the sun always burned them, and the crops did so well that there was money and to spare for everyone. They flew back to their youth for solace, trying to recapture lustiness and the hot blood leaping in their veins that had seemed to bring the sun nearer.

The old men were incurably romantic, and I was saddened hearing their thin voices battering at the door of memory. They are great story-tellers, often – like Mahmud – recounting their adventures with wit. The memory of Güzel is always with them, and every tragic love story takes colour from her tragedy, every young heroine borrows some of her ageless beauty. So it was with a story an old man told in that quiet hour while we waited for the women to call us to eat. At first I paid little attention to him for he seemed to be talking about marriage in a general way, saying that not all marriages gave happiness to the parents of the bride. He was silent for a long time and then he started his story.

In his youth a Yürük of his tribe had fallen in love with a girl from a tribe on the other side of Karadağ. In vain had his father and his elder brothers pleaded with the parents of the girl to give her to him. They refused always, at first with politeness, then with abuse, then with stones, and never would they give a reason for their refusal.

They set her four brothers to guard her and the poor young man never caught as much as a glimpse of the sole of her foot. Despair paled his cheek, unsteadied his hand when he was out shooting, and turned him away from his food. He loved her to distraction and pined away from lack of her.

One evening he stole into the girl's camp, and lying hidden in the bushes, watched his loved one preparing the evening meal, noting her pallor and her deep and heavy sighs. His heart bled for her, but not a word could he utter for her four brothers would have choked the life out of him there and then. His eyes followed her everywhere, and at nightfall, concealed by the darkness, he passed beside her, muttering as he passed that she was to have courage, he was here with her, later he would come for her. He found her father's tent, and lay hidden again until dead of night, when not even a dog barked, nor footfall fell. Creeping along the side of the tent where his beloved slept, he lifted the edge of the tent gently three times, as a signal to her that he was ready, but so gently did he lift it and let it fall again that had anyone else in the tent been awake they might have thought it was the wind.

Presently the girl came out from the tent, stealing out like a ghost, her face as pale as death. Together the young man and she hurried over the mountain to the spot, far away, where his horse was tethered. Like the wind they galloped to Karadağ, the young man's heart bursting for joy and the horse under him as fleet as the wings of the morning.

On Karadağ the girl was given into the care of the *oba bey*, for this was an affair of honour, maybe of death, and the young man could not touch her until the parents had been asked once more for their consent. The next evening the four brothers of the girl arrived, with other men from her tribe, and all of them were armed from top to toe. They demanded the girl, but the *oba bey* refused to hand her over, telling the brothers to go back and ask their father's consent once more.

The next evening they were back again, the father with them this time, and once more they demanded the girl. Fighting broke out between the two tribes but the *oba bey* held the father hostage, forbidding the shedding of blood. Seeing that he was defeated, and his daughter compromised in any case, the father gave his consent, saying that the marriage should take place then and there, and that the bridal pair should promise to live apart from the rest of the tribe. At this, the *oba bey* knew that it was intended to kill the young couple together. Yürük custom is simple and implacable. The young man had violated a family's honour and must die for his impertinence; the girl, however innocent, had to die too, for as long as she lived she would be a disfigurement on the family name. It was as final as that.

However, the *oba bey* said to the father and the four brothers, letting them see that he knew their intention, 'Whoever lays one hand on them in enmity will be killed with a bullet through his heart. The girl is ours now.'

The marriage was performed there and then, a few women being called up from their beds to assist the girl. The ceremony was performed by the light of oil lamps, only the faces of the few within the circle of yellow light visible. The girl's father and her four brothers rode back over the mountains, having said not a word to the girl. For several months afterwards the *oba bey* set men to guard their tent by night in case of attack. Many times during the first three months, one or other of the brothers would try and outwit the guards, seeking to take away his sister. But after a time they came no more and the people of Karadağ grew lax in their guard. The young couple were more in love than ever before, and as the days passed the young girl seemed to grow more beautiful and people heard her singing about the camp.

One day, a messenger brought the news that her mother was dying and wished to see her daughter once more before she died. The messenger brought the news too that his tribe offered the people of Karadağ a truce. The *oba bey*, anxious to see that the girl came to no harm, accompanied her and the messenger to her tribe.

He was received there with hospitality but reserve, saw for himself that the mother was indeed ill, and took a meal in the father's tent. Unspoken enmity was shown him, however, for his host led him to be seated in the 'place of the warrior', while he himself sat in the 'place of the neighbours'. The next morning, the *oba bey* returned to Karadağ, and no sooner was he away from the enemy camp than the mother sat up and in a hearty voice demanded food, declaring that such play-acting had famished her.

The girl was kept a prisoner and was not returned to Karadağ. War was now declared between the two tribes. They raided each other and the demented young husband continually sought an opportunity to get his wife back. The days and the weeks and the months dragged on, and still the girl was a prisoner. Then one day the *oba bey* received a messenger who had been sent by the mother to say that the girl was pining away for sight of her husband and to beg the *oba bey* to free her. At first, he was suspicious and rejected the messenger. Then a young woman came to the camp, with a lock of the girl's hair, and the *oba bey* knew that the mother was in need of his help, for a lock of hair is a plea for mercy in Yürük custom.

Many strong men were gathered together, including the old man who was telling the story, and they rode off one morning early, swearing they would bring back the girl by nightfall. The young husband rode at their head. When they arrived at the other camp fighting broke out at once, and the husband was sent in search of his wife. They were reunited with each other, she weeping in his arms for joy. In the moment of their embrace, however, before they even had time to run for safety, her eldest brother shot the young man through the back, piercing his lungs. Blood spattered over the arms and the dress of the girl and she fell with him to the ground, dragged down by the weight of his dying body. She was brought back to Karadağ, along with the body of her husband, but after a few months she pined away and died too, and they buried her beside him. Only in death were they able to be united for ever.

The old man sighed, finishing his story on a querulous note. I sighed too, affected by this saga of youth and beauty and death. It is only the young who have legends built about them, and as memories fade and the people who knew them grow older, their story takes on an epic quality. No heroine has ever been thought plain after her death.

The sky was quite dark now and a chilly night breeze had sprung up, eddying the dust about our feet. And I thought that this great open space on the mountain had witnessed many events of life and death. The earth was saturated with the blood of all the heroes of Yürük tales, with the tears of their heroines; did nothing remain? Could not a trick of atmosphere deceive one into thinking that shadows walked among us? Why were they always sad tales they told, where violence triumphed, never pity? Did the clue to their personalities lie in the stories they told? I shivered, but not with the cold.

That night we ate in the *oba bey*'s tent. The good smell of partridge made me hungry, and when at last a bird was borne in on a bed of *pilav*, I fell on it like a wolf, already an adept at eating with my hands. After coffee had been served in our honour, and water poured over our hands in an attempt to cleanse them, neighbours began to crowd in.

Soon the tent, large as it was, was packed. Candles threw circles of yellow light on dark faces, smoke rose from the fire, and, sitting cross-legged, I was conscious of how my whole body ached from the day's long ride. Musicians came in, summoned in out of the darkness to play their wild lonely music for our delectation. Mahmud sang us a warrior's song in his quavering, centenarian voice. A boy danced for us, but not in the erotic manner of the plains. His dancing was a shuffling affair, demanding ingenious footwork and a good deal of twirling, reminiscent of the Dervishes. His body shivered in time to the wild music and he was like something out of a crazy dream. Thus might the warriors of Genghis Khan have danced about their campfires.

Afterwards he did a sword dance, which I had once seen in Diyar-bekır. The Yürük version of the sword dance, however, was more savage and I found it difficult to keep from flinching when he came running at me with the sword pointed directly at my throat. He leaped and bounded in the small dancing space, his black hair falling across his eyes, his stamping feet kicking up a cloud of dust that threatened to put out the candles. The music throbbed rhythmically, almost hypnotically. The ferocious young dancer flashed his swords, sharpening them one against the other in time with the music, then bounding across the room in a graceful leap to thrust a sword through an imaginary heart or to brandish it only a millimetre or so from the brown throats of the onlookers. I felt a dampness along the back of my neck. The music and the uninhibited savagery of the dancing took me back to a time when the power of the sword was everything.

The victims selected for the ordeal of having a sharp sword within a hair's breadth of their unprotected throats were unmoved, rolling their cigarettes phlegmatically even while the swords flashed reflected fire just above them. Having faced the ordeal once, I hoped I should not be called upon to do so again. In any case, I flinched for the men singled out. I stole a glance at Dursun Bey who was chewing melon seeds and looking perfectly composed. Beyond him, Hikmet Bey was gazing at the dancer, entranced.

The dancing over, and the fire of ecstasy gone from his face, the boy looked shy and dull. Only music and the lust of the savage had transformed him into something wild and splendid.

The music now grew grave and sad, full of the nostalgia of the nomads themselves. The listening faces were impassive, however. It was impossible to know them, to assess them or romanticise over them. Perhaps they were nothing more than lazy good-for-nothings. Perhaps their nomadism was a form of cretinism.

Bidding the *oba bey* good-night, we rose from our cramped positions and slipped over the dew-laden grass to our tent. For a time I stood outside, breathing in the cold air. Except for the laughter of the men which could still be heard from the *oba bey*'s tent, everywhere was silent, wrapped in mystery.

A soft dark shape came up beside me, and a donkey put his face against my arm. We nuzzled each other for a few minutes in silence but when I went into the tent he set up such a plaintive hee-hawing that I was forced to go outside again to quieten him. His muzzle felt soft and wet and rough against my skin and I couldn't get rid of him. I was rescued at last by Dursun Bey who gave the donkey the sharp slap on the nose which I hadn't had the heart to give and which sent him clattering away between the tents, his cries seeming to register sorrow rather than anger against me.

I lay down guiltily to sleep.

8

Women's Work – Herb Medicines and Superstitions –
Childbirth – Black and White Magic – Jinn

TO THE OUTSIDER, life in a Yürük camp verged on the ideal. There were no trains to catch, no bills to pay, no social conscience to be deferred to. On the surface it was perfect. But then, as Cemal pointed out, we were guests; it made all the difference. For the Yürük himself life was a hazard, albeit a hazard which he met with cheerfulness.

The day started at cockcrow. Summer or winter, water had to be fetched long distances. This was done by the women who carried it in enormous goatskin jars on shoulder yokes, generally supporting a baby on their back as well. It was the women also who journeyed to the forests, a day's journey away from camp, to bring home the wood left behind by the men. The men never brought back any more than they could help, and what they did bring back was tied into bundles and sold in the valleys.

The women who remained in camp were generally old, and it was left to them to milk the sheep and the goats, do the family washing – in vast zinc-lined wooden tubs – and prepare the meals. They also made the butter and cheese. Butter was made in goatskin bags slung between two poles, a long stick being thrust into the milk and plunged up and down until the butter formed. As the goatskin bags are seldom thoroughly clean, Yürük butter is always slightly rancid, and very unpleasant until one has acquired the taste.

Women, even when gossiping, never seemed idle. There was always something being worked or mended in their hands – a thick white woollen stocking for a husband or son, a new camel-hair rug to replace a worn-out one, a pair of trousers already patched innumerable times. Even when they were going to fetch water or leading a camel down to winter quarters, the women spun and wove tirelessly. With the right hand they twisted the thread of wool or hair and with the left hand they drew from the distaff. The stone weighting the thread, sometimes nothing more than a lump of clay, is the same as their ancestors used in neolithic times. To see a Yürük woman weaving as she walks, her hands almost a separate part of her, is to be aware less of the passage of time than of the unchanging nature of the Yürük themselves. She is ageless, monumental, passing through the centuries with her black-haired children and her big-booted, talkative men.

There are no medical facilities for the Yürük people. They are too remotely placed to merit visits from doctors sent out by Ankara, and in any case would probably scorn orthodox medicines. While I was with them, three men returned from the forest, one of them with his foot almost severed. While felling trees his axe had slipped, plunging through his stout boot and cutting through the flesh to the bone. His one concern when he returned seemed to be that he had ruined the newly knitted socks his wife had made for him! His face was grey with fatigue and pain, but he never once mentioned his injury and submitted to the ministrations of the women with sly jokes. The emergency treatment his comrades had used in the forest was raw tobacco. This they had pressed down on the foot in great wads, bandaging it with a bit of rag. It took them two whole days to make camp, and when the rag and the foul mess of tobacco was removed the wound was found to be crawling with maggots. These were cleaned out with what seemed to me nearly boiling water, so that my own flesh quaked for his discomfort, and then dressed with a variety of mosses. Before we left the camp the wound was almost healed.

Wise Women, to whom the secret of herbal remedies is passed

down from one generation to another, are to be found in nearly all Yürük camps. Whatever the treatment is, however, it is preceded by readings from the Koran, coupled with shamanistic ritual. Faith-healing and the laying on of hands is common practice. In some cases, the healer reads from the Koran and then blows forty-one-and-a-half times on the affected spot, allegedly blowing away the evil spirits. It is not known why this number is chosen.

No point is gained by debating why these methods have so much success; the fact is that they *work*, whether auto-suggestion comes into it or not. In cases of acute inflammation, camel dung is powdered, again with ritual, and applied to the inflammation. The patient is wrapped in cloths perfumed with herbs and at the end of three days is unwrapped in front of a blazing fire, cured. The fumes of powdered rue are held to be good for febrile conditions and – when it is obtainable – a piece of shroud from a dead body is burned and the patient made to inhale the smoke. The scalp of a newly dead infant is said to be a certain cure for persistent migraine and certain forms of epilepsy. Verbena juice is rubbed on the back and chest of a person spitting blood, and the leaves and flowers of the yellow coltsfoot are brewed for asthma and bronchial complaints. The bitter root of the bog-flower is gathered beside streams and used for rheumatic complaints and as a tonic for young people growing too fast. A form of wild geranium, a low-growing bright-red plant, is gathered in the valleys to make a salve for wounds, and a brew from it is said to relieve internal haemorrhage.

Even less orthodox is the practice of breathing upon an open wound, inscribing with the fingers Arabic symbols spelling the name of the Prophet. Lead, said to have invaluable properties against the Evil Eye, is dropped into boiling water, acquiring strange shapes; accompanied by incantations, it is believed to cure even the most obstinate state of bewitchedness. Toothache, when not treated by herbal remedy, is treated by praying over a pinch of salt sprinkled on a nail driven into a stake. The nail is then removed, placed against the aching tooth and then carried in the sufferer's turban until the toothache is cured. On the whole, however,

Yürük teeth are excellent. This is probably due to the fact that they clean their teeth with salt rubbed on with their fingers, perhaps arresting infection at its source.

Tooth extraction is somewhat more painful. In less bad cases, a pair of pliers is used – not always successfully, and then the unfortunate victim is hurried down the mountain, bellowing with pain, face swollen to twice its normal size, and the Karaman barber takes over the torture. A present of eggs is given him for his trouble, but if the present is large enough and the victim a case for a higher authority, such as the uncertified dentist found in nearly every Turkish village, an injection is given and a bigger pair of pliers used. Another method of tooth extraction is to tie a long piece of wire to the aching tooth, fasten the other end to a stout post and then chase the victim round and round the post with a bundle of burning rags held near the seat of his pants. The fear of being burned makes the sufferer temporarily forget his aching tooth and run from the flame in ever widening circles until a tightening of the wire and a sharp stab of pain tells him the tooth is out. This doesn't *always* work, of course.

Internal pains which persist are treated, externally I believe, although I wouldn't be certain of this, with a mixture of wild honey and dog's excrement. The blood of a black goat and chicken embryos are cures for sterility in the male. In some tribes, snakes are kept for divination as well as curative purposes. I was glad there were none on Karadağ. I was told that the snake-charmer knows each snake by name. It seems that they come when they are called and at the snake-charmer's bidding curl themselves about a patient's neck or stomach. Leeches are used for blood-letting, and I saw a small pale child lying out under the sun, with leeches clinging to his naked body, swollen and repulsive, while an older child picked them off now and then with expert hand.

Great use is made of religious charms, which are written on pieces of paper. It is nothing for an ailing old man to carry half a dozen such charms. The efficacy of prayer is well known to the Yürük and, indeed, no treatment is ever started until prayers have been said. The amazing thing is that these illiterate people are able to execute the Arabic symbols so faithfully and delicately, and the Wise Women can recite the Koran by heart, knowing which *surah* is effective in which illness.

Childbirth, however, is a matter of luck, and regarded as a natural function, with no fuss attached to it. If a mother is strong, giving birth is often over in a few minutes; if she is weak she very likely dies, the baby too.

During our second week with the Yürük, we were invited one evening to eat with one Ismet, a fairly well-to-do tribesman who owned many sheep. It was a chilly evening, more like March than August, and the men had been prophesying an early winter. Candles dispelled some of the gloom in the dark tent. A young boy brought in a bowl of maize soup. Our host was plainly uneasy, and kept going outside where we could hear him talking in a low voice to someone else. Once Hikmet Bey asked if there was anything wrong but he said there wasn't, adding something about the sheep not having been milked yet.

It was another hour before we heard the familiar tinkle of the sheep bells, and at once our host jumped up and went outside. He returned after a short interval and we asked him once again if there was anything the matter.

'Everything is all right now,' he said, his voice much more cheerful than it had been all the evening. 'The sheep are being milked now. Their udders are bursting but my daughter-in-law is attending them. She was late bringing them home and I was afraid an accident had happened to one of them in the dark. She gave birth to a child on the way.'

This latter remark was so unexpected that for a few moments I wasn't sure I had heard aright. I asked him if he had said she'd given birth, and he replied that he had. Soon afterwards the young woman came into the tent with two cans of milk in her hands and the newborn infant strapped on her back. I could hardly believe my eyes. Nobody took the slightest notice of her or offered to help her, and I was too afraid of having my actions misinterpreted to do anything. Next morning at dawn she was off again, taking the sheep to pasturage.

The *oba bey*, when I mentioned the matter, shrugged his shoulders and seemed astonished at my concern. He said that most of the women gave birth in their tents but that there was nothing unusual, although it didn't happen very frequently, about giving birth on the mountain. The *oba bey* knew very little about the death rate for mother and child, but thought it might be as high as thirty per cent in summer, somewhat higher in winter. 'But Allah is merciful,' he added. 'If they didn't go that way they'd go some other, and if they didn't go at all where would we be? How would we feed them all?'

When I next saw Ismet's daughter-in-law, the baby was still strapped on her back, and wearing a blue bead about its neck to protect it from the Evil Eye. Some of these beads are very beautiful and have been handed down in families for centuries. The beads that the Yürük value most, and these they will not part with, are mottled, more grey than blue, except in certain lights when the blue shines through milkily, with exquisite veining. Hikmet Bey said they were rock quartz, worn smooth with constant handling.

Superstition is rife among them, and even the flight of a bird has its omens. The Wise Woman, adept at breaking spells, can also cast them, and this makes her greatly respected, perhaps even feared. Nobody, least of all the Wise Woman, knows why these spells work; they know the method but not the reason.

There was an old man on Karadağ, a shaman, who, in an argument with Dursun Bey, told him that if he wished he could root him to the spot where he was standing. He was a gentle-looking old man but Dursun Bey was taking no chances and declined to be a guinea pig. Hikmet Bey called the old man's bluff and stepped forward in the place of Dursun Bey. He was very jocular about it.

'He'll try and hypnotise me,' he explained to us with a wink. 'They practise these tricks on each other and probably they work because they're all steeped in superstition, but you'll see it'll have no effect at all on an educated mind.'

He went up to the shaman confidently.

'Please sit down,' said the shaman. 'You are in no danger from me – as you said, what can a poor old man like me do to you?'

Hikmet sat on a stone looking somewhat disappointed. They talked for a time, the old man refusing to be drawn about the spells he was said to be able to cast. After a time he turned away to his tent and we called to Hikmet to join us, but Hikmet's face was the colour of chalk and in a strangled voice he said that he couldn't move. Not believing him, Dursun Bey and I went up to him and pulled him by his arms. He stood up at once.

'There!' I said. 'Auto-suggestion, Hikmet Bey. You're as bad as any of them here. You tried to pretend you weren't afraid of the shaman, and then your own mind worked on you instead.'

'I swear it wasn't that,' Hikmet said uneasily. 'My body felt like a ton of bricks. I *couldn't* move!'

'Of course you couldn't because your own mind was playing tricks on you.'

The shaman joined us. 'You think I could not do it?' he asked me.

'I don't think anything of the kind. I don't know what you can do and what you can't do, but I find it difficult to believe that your power is as great as the power of Hikmet Bey's own mind. He *himself* willed his body not to move.'

The old man's eyes held mine for a second or two and then he bowed, one hand on his breast, and moved away. I must confess I was relieved he hadn't taken it into his head to root *me* to the spot!

Osman, who was with us, was disturbed by my attitude. He said I had insulted the shaman and would surely pay for it, and at this a twinge of fear slid through my mind. I dismissed the thought, however, and told Osman that it was difficult for city people to be credulous.

Osman said his grandmother had been a shaman and that once from a distance of six kilometres she had freed a goat that had become entangled in some thorn bushes. She had 'seen' the goat, and had informed her family that the goat's udder was torn. She commanded one of the women to go and free the goat immediately, and in the meantime she herself would 'breathe' on the wound so that the goat wouldn't die. It was Osman's mother who had been sent after the goat, and after searching for nearly two hours she found it entangled in thorn bushes, badly lacerated and unable to move.

She coaxed it back to the camp where the shaman smeared the wound with herb ointment; thereupon, to everyone's surprise, the goat bounded into the air, cured instantaneously. I questioned Osman's use of the word 'surprise' for, I said, if they were so certain that the shaman could perform such deeds, and indeed expected her to do so, why were they so surprised. Osman grew sulky at this, and finally produced his mother who said she remembered the incident but not the instantaneous cure. According to her, the shaman had not used any ointment but had merely 'breathed' on the wound and inscribed Arabic symbols over it. Hot dispute broke out between mother and son but it was eventually agreed that even if the cure hadn't been as quick as Osman said it was, nevertheless the goat was back at pasture the next day.

This story indicated that shamans are clairvoyant as well as everything else. They are very powerful in the tribes, and even an *oba bey* is careful never to fall foul of them.

That night, unable to sleep immediately, I lay for a time staring up at a patch of star-filled sky that showed through a hole in the tent. I was tranquil, had eaten well, and was thinking of the next stage of my travels, for it would soon be time to leave the Yürük and descend to the valleys again. For a while I meditated on the life of the nomads, almost envying them their splendid isolation and toying with the idea of remaining with them until winter came.

The night was hot and sleep far away. A movement across my chest distracted my thoughts and I raised my hand to investigate – or perhaps I should say I *attempted* to raise my hand, for to my astonishment I couldn't move it. Furthermore, there was no feeling in it, or in the arm. It was ridiculous but I was paralysed down one side, for I found I couldn't move my right leg either! Busy investigating this new sensation, or rather lack of sensation, I forgot all about the legion of fleas that were making inroads on my chest. I tried to call Cemal, but I couldn't speak. Had I had a stroke? Did hale and hearty men of forty-five have strokes? The amazement passed away to be replaced with a sort of panic. I was really frightened, although I tried to fight this feeling. However, it was all very well telling myself everything was fine and that I was only numbed by my manner of lying, it was another thing to make myself believe it. After all, I had been lying on my *back*!

Added to this was the discomfort of the fleas. They explored the hairs of my chest, they investigated my neck and they burned their way like red-hot needles along my back. It was very unpleasant; there was I, supine on my straw bed, unable to help myself. I sat up with difficulty, for one half of me had to lift the other half, and it was like lifting a ton of bricks. The sensation was so odd I had to lie down again.

I was really alarmed, not least by the fact that I couldn't even draw my companions' attention to my plight. I felt myself begin to sweat with terror. By this time I was as rigid as a corpse. I couldn't even feel the fleas any more. I tried to pray but I was too terrified to think properly. The existence of God seemed impossibly remote, His care for me woefully lax. I let fear ride me and waited for my death. I don't know how long I remained in this pitiable state but there came a time when I grew angry, when I said to myself: I *will* move. This was a fallacy, however. I didn't move. I remained as stiff as yesterday's corpse. In the midst of all this unbelievable mental turmoil the face of the shaman was suddenly before me. I think we stared at each other for a long time. Presently the illusion faded and I was able to sit up again.

My heart was thumping painfully and I was as tired as if I had fought a mighty battle. I felt for my torch and snapped it on, Cemal grunting at the sudden spurt of light. I shone the torch over my naked body and picked off two lice. I felt sick. I was filled with loathing for camp life and my romantic notions. And then I felt homesick. I wanted to be with my family, not in any specified time but there and then. I wanted to live like a civilised human being. Here I was in a musty tent where fleas and bugs multiplied with ferocity and lice clung to my body. I was dirty and lousy, and I had been put under a spell by an even dirtier, even lousier old shaman to teach me a lesson for doubting him.

I pulled on my trousers and a woollen sweater and went out into the night. The camp lay sleeping, silent and eerie. The tents were dark humps against a barely lighter skyline, and silence and the high, bright moon seemed to have signed a pact with each other. The night was full of the smell of the dew-wet earth, and I leaned against the tent, full of inexpressible longings, a prey to a nostalgia for my family that had never before attacked me in quite the same way.

The next morning I picked several more lice off my shirt, feeling sick every time I killed one of them – not out of compunction but from loathing. Osman was very much amused by my squeamishness.

'Lice?' he said to me. 'Why, brother, we've bred them all our lives!'

After we had eaten – fried eggs, honey, goat's cheese and *sebit* – we were told that the *oba bey* wanted to talk to us. We found him outside his tent, staring into space. When he saw us he stood up, put his hands on our shoulders in turn and said: 'My brothers, you are now one of us. You have been with us long enough not to be guests any more. I beg you to remain with us as long as you wish, even for the rest of your lives. We give you the tent for your own and the oldest among you should take the "place of the warrior". If you wish you may work with us, or you may do nothing at all but sit in the sun.'

This was very handsome of him but we were inclined to believe that he wanted to be rid of us. Hikmet Bey, mentioning this aspect jokingly, offended Osman who at once defended the noble sentiments of his *oba bey*.

Once upon a time, said Osman, before he was born, a stranger came to Karadağ. He was made welcome by the *oba bey* of that time, and after a certain period he was told, as we had been, that now he had been with them long enough to be regarded as one of themselves. The stranger was a young man then, and he chose to make his life among them. He hunted with the men, and sometimes went to the forest with them. In winter he descended the mountain to Binbirkilise (the Thousand and One Churches), and in the course of time he even learned how to make rush baskets and sell them in Karaman. All this time the tribe knew him only by the name he had told them to call him. They did not know where he had come from or why he had made his life among them, and they never asked, for that would have been an abuse of privacy.

The *oba bey* became old and died and was replaced by his son. The son was struck by lightning in the prime of his life and was replaced by *his* son. This new *oba bey* had a ten-year-old son who one day asked the stranger where he had come from. The *oba bey* heard his son asking this question and reproved him angrily: 'Neither your grandfather nor your great-grandfather asked such a question,' he said. 'Why do you?'

'So you see,' said Osman crossly, 'we are people like that. Our guests are sent by God. If they stay with us it is because God wishes it. We have no right to ask questions, or turn them away.'

Hikmet Bey said he was very sorry.

I went in search of the shaman. He was sitting outside his tent eating a bowl of yoghurt to which pounded garlic had been added. The stench was abominable. He greeted me unsmilingly but made room for me to sit beside him. He finished his yoghurt, not talking, and I grew sulkier and sulkier, wondering why I had sought him out at all. I decided, somewhat haughtily, that I had no intention of baring my mind to him. He startled me when he said: 'Pride is the enemy of truth, my son.'

'Was it you last night?' I asked.

He passed the empty bowl to a child and turned to face me. 'You had doubted me,' he said.

'But you have no right to set yourself up as God,' I replied crossly. 'What right have you to presume to teach me a lesson?'

He bowed his head for a moment. 'I am not always humble,' he answered.

We stared at each other. His white hair showed in curled tufts from under his black cap, his yellow cheeks were sucked in. He was more Mongoloid in appearance than most Yürük, and his body too was thin and light so that he was a little like the pictures one sees of Chinese mandarins. He only needed a drooping moustache to complete the picture.

'You are able to read letters and write with a pen,' he said, 'but that does not mean that you are able to understand everything in this life. Your friends say that you write books. What is a book? I have never seen one.'

'You have seen the Koran,' I replied.

'Ah, so! The Koran is a book. You write a book like the Koran, then surely you must be a very great *hoca*?'

'No, no,' I said, his simplicity disarming me. 'But you said you had never seen a book, and I wanted to say that the Koran, which is also a book, and which you have seen, is what is meant when they say I write books.' This had even become involved for me; I couldn't hope he would understand.

'The Koran,' he retorted disapprovingly, 'is God's holy word. How can you write anything like that?'

There was a long silence, during which he took a handful of melon seeds from his pocket, offered me some which I declined, then started chewing some himself.

'I find it impossible to explain,' I said, 'what I mean by a book. It has pages like the Koran, it has writings in it, but they are writings out of my own head.'

'Oh, ho!' he chuckled. 'You too set yourself up as God. Only God makes books.'

He was shabby and unlettered. He had the gentlest face I had ever seen. Some inner tranquillity radiated from him. He was like a man who had spent his life communing with God.

'Show me your hand,' he said suddenly, and when I held out my left hand he waved it away, then took my right hand in his and looked at the palm deeply.

'There is much coming and going,' he said, 'and much water. You were born with water in your sign and you will be happy if you live near it.' He sighed heavily and I thought he was going to tell me something calamitous. I had the feeling he already knew my future. 'Many people will follow you,' he said. 'They will know your name. You will have much honour. You will die in a far country but not the country you have come from. Your Guardian Angel has much power over you, you will live a long time, but fire is your enemy. You must beware of fire.' He let go my hand. 'I will pray for your safety,' he said.

It was the first time anyone had prophesied my future. I wished to believe the things he said, if only because they were pleasant. I asked him how he could read the future, but his answers were unsatisfactory. He said he saw pictures. He couldn't tell me why, neither could he explain what he saw. He used simple words like 'movement' and 'water' or 'fire'.

'But perhaps they're just thoughts in your head,' I suggested. 'If I close my eyes, for instance, I can make pictures too.'

He smiled patiently. He had said all he could. If I were so stupid as to believe I could see pictures as well . . .

'Try and tell me,' I said.

'There is a shaking in my head,' he answered, 'that is movement. When I looked at your hand there was too much shaking inside me. I was dizzy with it. There are people in a line, like we Yürük when we take our camels and go down Karadağ in winter. What else can I say? These are people following something. I saw people following you. Then a great flame leaped up in my mind and I knew that there was danger for you in fire.'

I desisted. It was like torturing a child with adult questions, trying to make the child reply in adult language. This shaman knew he had a power, he knew what that power could do, but he had no idea where it came from. He spoke without pride. He was too simple, too sure of himself, for pride.

Many times during our conversation he beat his breast, asking God's forgiveness for bewitching me. 'I was sinful,' he wailed. 'I thought to humble your pride by elevating my own.' And once again he called on God to punish him, to cut out his tongue, to blind him, to paralyse him. His simplicity was the barrier between us for I was impatient with his beliefs, his outbursts of sorrow. His peasant speech was difficult to follow, and it was overladen with phrases from the Koran, mystically poetic but difficult to understand. He had no reasoning powers at all. He took it for granted that he could cure people of illness or, working on a lower plane, bewitch them. He was not curious, and reproved me for asking so many questions.

'I have sought nothing,' he said. 'I am as God made me. I do not question God.'

He would not discuss religion with me either, holding up his hands in real horror when I questioned Mohammed's authority or right to invest his son-in-law, Ali, with the mantle of the Prophet.

'All men meet at the top of the mountain,' he said somewhat ambiguously and with a tone of finality.

He gave me a blue bead. It was oval shaped and translucent. He said it was the stone the Yürük people called the Eye of God.

'This will protect you,' he said, and I believed him, letting the pretty stone lie in my hand for a moment or two, still warm from his pocket and his own belief.

We talked of other shamans, but only disjointedly, for he did not want to discuss them. He did say, however, that they didn't always use their 'magic' for good purposes. They were in league with Şeytan (Satan), he said, and the jinn helped them to perpetrate their evil intentions. Some of these shamans could even change their shape when darkness fell, and this was the time when they committed their wickedest deeds. They stole young virgins from their fathers' tents, despoiling them. They drew the living spirit out of others, leaving them witless – 'empty as the summer sky', the shaman called it. They caused sickness, death and pestilence. Sometimes men hired them to kill their enemy from a distance. He would not say how this was done but admitted it was not always sudden; sometimes a man lingered on for days, even months, his strength ebbing from him 'with every cock that crew'. They were even able to bewitch animals, sometimes making a flock of ewes run dry while their own flocks flowed over with milk. He said their powers were greater than his own, for he only practised 'white magic', but that very often God let the devil prevail as a punishment to mankind. When I remonstrated that this was rather hard on the innocent victims, he said sententiously that all was clear in God's mind; His Eyes, he added, saw everything at once, nothing was hidden from Him and only He knew the end of a journey.

I discovered that for all his piety and his belief in the superior power of God, he himself was not immune from worldly fret. He was afraid of the dark. He thought that the moon was a beautiful demon 'set up there in God's garden to delude and snare men'.

'The moon is the Devil's agent,' he said. 'She is the weed in the heavenly gardens. She tempts men to sleep under her evil light, and then the Devil comes along and takes away the mind.'

But he regarded the jinn as more evil, for whereas the moon was predictable, and big enough to be seen anywhere on earth, you never knew where you were with the jinn, and one could never be sure what shapes they would take. He called them the 'bad men of the invisible world', and when I asked him about the invisible world he said that this was the twin of our own world, impinging on us everywhere. I thought this was a remarkably sophisticated attitude to take.

The Yürük is very afraid of the jinn. No Yürük will ever cross dirty water without first calling on Allah to protect him, then blowing with his breath three times to scatter the jinn. Neither can he throw some un-wanted thing – a scrap of paper, the leavings of a meal – out into the night. Night is the realm of the jinn and whatever is thrown out might injure one of them. Their revenge will be swift, maybe fatal. A man might break his ankle, his arm, his leg, become paralysed; a fire may burn down his tent, a high wind injure his sheep. And it's too late to say your prayers *after* you have injured a jinn. You should have thought of that before, and now you must take what the Devil sends. The shaman said that Mohammed is supposed to have converted the wickedest of the jinn to Islam, but there are many others to do damage.

Jinn have been known to come up on a man as a faint light, growing larger as the distance decreases. When they are quite close to each other, the light grows to monstrous proportions, displaying the head of a toad and the body of a goat with the eerie light outlining the whole apparition in awful brilliance. No man has ever seen this terrible manifestation and escaped unscathed. Some are beaten senseless. Some die at once, the sight too much for them. Others are rendered witless, spending the rest of their days in vacant wandering, feared and shunned by all, for the power of the dreadful light is said to be still in their eyes.

There are jinn who guard the cemeteries and often these take the forms of owls or bats. A Yürük was found dead the year before last in the cemetery the other side of the mountain. When he was discovered there was a large white owl gliding over him, and the owl attacked the men who were trying to bury their dead comrade.

Sometimes a jinnee took the form of a beautiful moon maiden, lying in wait for the men coming back from the forest. Usually she became visible to only one of the men, and with beckoning gestures she lured him on, always keeping a little ahead of him, her perfect form showing through the flimsy draperies of her dress. The besotted man would follow her over hill and dale until he reached the place where the other jinn were waiting to feast on human flesh. The maiden would disappear, dissolving in the moonlight – some had even been seen flitting up a moonbeam to their home in the sky – and the jinn would fall upon the man.

The shaman was so sincere in his beliefs, and so persuasive, that for the rest of the time we were in camp I never dared throw anything out of the tent at night. Thus are legends given substance.

9

Yürük Dress Customs – Mainly about Women –
Marriage – Symbolic Language – the Karadag Bear

O N ONE DAY of each week the women gathered round a vast, field-type oven to make the family bread. Breadmaking is a social affair, and for the Yürük women takes the place of the *hamam* gatherings of the Ottoman Empire.

For breadmaking the Yürük women don bright dresses and their best headgear. What with butter-making, fetching water, going to the forest, tending sheep and so on, they do not have much time for exchanging confidences: but the day they make bread compensates for all this. Marriageable girls, and sons, are discussed. A little scandal is passed around – perhaps a young widow is showing, by the headscarf she wears, that she is on the marriage market again. The older women do not care for this, since their daughters' chances may be ruined. The daughters do not approve either since the widow is generally pretty, free in her manners and separated from the virgins by experience. She moves with assurance, knows how to talk with her eyes and makes the young girls seem gauche by contrast.

The finer the breadmaking morning is, the greater the chatter and the laughter. Husbands are in the forest cutting down trees, away on a hunting expedition or working in the fields. Relaxed and free, the women hurry to and fro, children crawling on the sun-baked earth. Mothers scold good-naturedly, young girls fetch flour and overflowing buckets of spring water, the drops splashing on the parched earth, dried by the fierce sun before they scarcely have time to stain it. The old women, past experts at breadmaking and gossip, assume positions of eminence and authority near the oven, advising, criticising, inviolate.

The sudden emergence of so many coloured headscarves is in striking contrast to the dull ones worn on ordinary days. The *oba bey*'s mother, who took me under her wing, explained the meaning of the scarves, their 'language' really, which is recognised by every Yürük man and woman, no matter from which tribe they come. It was a fascinating lesson, and the women themselves, watching with bright eyes and cheeks flushed from stooping over the fire, were like rare flowers set down unexpectedly among the drab tents on Karadağ.

One old woman wore her full traditional dress. The *oba bey*'s mother explained that this was in my honour. She sat a little apart from the breadmakers, serene and resplendent, her old hands folded on her lap, stiff looking in her brilliant voluminous dress which was embroidered in gold and silver thread, a little tarnished now from age. Silk ribbons were threaded through her hair which, despite her years, was only faintly streaked with grey. From a circlet of gold above her forehead several gold coins depended. On her feet were Moorish-type slippers.

Her head covering, a *dalfez*, was bound turban-wise with a black silk scarf. This showed she was a widow and, because her hair was unplaited, had no wish to marry again. This is one of the instances where Yürük women differ greatly from the Turkish women of the plains. A Yürük widow finds no difficulty in marrying again and has no false pride about showing her wishes. The woman of the plains, when widowed, rarely finds a second husband. Neither would she be brave enough to seek one and bear the censure of her neighbours. The peasant and the townsman look for a virgin girl and would consider he had been insulted if he were offered a widow, no matter how young and pretty. But even virginity has its trials, for if a girl is betrothed and for any reason breaks her betrothal, even because of the death of the prospective bridegroom, she is doomed to spinsterhood. This rigid and unnatural tradition shows no sign of dying out.

Among the Yürük tribes, prostitutes are rare, and those there are are themselves usually the bastard daughters of prostitutes. I was told there were none on Karadağ, Osman looking faintly shocked that I should ask such a question. However, the fact that I had asked obviously worried him for the same day he came to me, and after a lot of ambiguous remarks, came out into the open with the offer of a young boy who would be willing to oblige me if ever I felt life was too hard to bear. Hikmet, who was with me, gladly offered to take my place at once, and strode off jauntily with Osman to an assignation which had been prepared for me.

However, prostitutes it seemed were not frowned upon too severely. In fact, one old woman told me with a cackle that when she was young there were many times when she would have been glad if her husband had sought his pleasure elsewhere. After a hard day in the fields, she said, and the rearing of seven children, she could have done with a little time off from love. The years may have softened her, however, or perhaps she only talked for the sake of talking, for younger women were less enthusiastic about the value of prostitutes. They showed no embarrassment in discussing them, but plenty of resentment.

The pleasant language of women's headgear was told me by two girls, with many little giggles and sidelong looks at each other and soft explosions of laughter always at my expense. All the women chattered incessantly, running to and fro with their flour and water, lifting expressive hands covered with dough, relating bits of gossip as it occurred to them, often with no sequence, their alert minds running ahead of their tripping tongues.

The subject of Yürük virility was a source of pleasure and pride. They told me the story of Orhan who was nearly as old as their beloved Mahmud. At the age of eighty-seven he had been married three times and had buried all his wives. They said he had twenty-one children, one hundred and five grandchildren and forty-three great-grandchildren.

They were almost a tribe in themselves. One day, Orhan confessed to his eldest son that he was lonely and couldn't sleep by himself any longer. He said he trembled with the cold at night and missed the feel of a woman beside him. In short, he said, he wanted another wife. The children and the grandchildren consulted together and decided that a certain widow they knew, who showed by the manner in which she plaited her hair that she wished for another husband, would make a good wife for the old man. She was thirty or so and, according to Yürük standards, good looking – and this they ranked as of great importance, for the old man himself had no use for a woman without looks.

When the woman was approached by the eldest son of the old man (the son himself was seventy), she at first mistook his proposal and thought it was he who wanted to marry her. She said she was willing. He explained it was his old father who wanted a wife. Showing no concern, she said she was still willing. The children and the grandchildren were very pleased with this news, and half a dozen of them hurried off to see the old man to tell him that his troubles were at an end. However, instead of being grateful to them for the trouble they had taken, he flew into a terrible rage, so terrible that they thought he would have a heart attack or burst a blood vessel. He told them he was capable of finding a bride for himself, and that if they thought he was going to marry an old woman of thirty they were very much mistaken. He wanted a young girl, he said, whether virgin or widow was all one to him, but she had to be *young*, and hot-blooded. Not only would she keep him warm at night but she would give him more children, and with a suggestive gesture he pointed to himself and said there was plenty of life in him yet. He added that he certainly wasn't going to squander it on a tough old widow.

Brushing up his beard with olive oil and setting his black *kaftan* at a rakish angle, he hobbled across to the tent of a neighbour. Here he said that he wanted to marry the neighbour's sixteen-year-old daughter. The proposal was accepted and he came away in triumph, gathered his large family around him and reminded them of the Turkish equivalent of faint heart never won fair maiden.

Orhan was married in due course and within the year he was presented with a fine son, a lusty infant weighing nearly twelve pounds. This proved to his neighbours that the wild shooting they had heard on his wedding night – each time he had made love to his wife he had shouted to his sons to let off another round of ammunition – marked not only the consummation of his marriage but the conception of his fine son as well. Four more sons were born to him before he died, and now the young widow was looking for another husband.

Yürük girls are sometimes very beautiful when young but lose their looks early on in marriage. They rarely lose their figures, for their active life keeps them lean. Many of the women in their thirties looked hard and muscular, however.

In the camp there were several young girls of about twelve or thirteen years old and a few of them were exquisite. I remember one of them in particular. She was not quite twelve. Her delicate oval face was the setting for a pair of large dark eyes that sparkled with laughter and was framed by black curls that barely reached her shoulders. The tender purity of her face was as heart-rending and as fresh as a spring morning. Her hands and feet were as delicately formed as those of a lady of breeding. Everything about her seemed fashioned on a diminutive scale and it was a pleasure to watch her talking, to note the tender play of her mobile mouth and the extraordinary delicacy of her flashing hands. She was already betrothed to a man more than twice her age. She had no freedom of choice, for her parents had arranged the marriage. If one day she fell in love with a man nearer her own age there was nothing she could do about it.

The penalty for adultery, or loss of virginity before marriage, is death. The seducer may escape even censure but for the girl it means death at the hands of a member of her own family. The Yürük says no woman can be taken against her wil and that it is through the women of the family that a man's honour is broken. Only death retrieves the honour. There is no compromise, and no sentimentality. The girl is killed swiftly, in cold blood. Afterwards the tribe shelters the killer, if need be, from the *jandarma*.

From the age of twelve onwards all Yürük girls have their hair plaited tightly and wear a special headdress. This consists of a sort of flat cap, bound with an embroidered silk scarf. The edges of the scarf are adorned with gold coins which tinkle captivatingly when she walks and denote the possible wealth of her father. Such a headdress means that the girl is ready for marriage, although not yet betrothed, and any young man is free to ask her parents' consent. There is no mistaking such a girl. When a white silk scarf is added to the embroidered scarf the girl is known to be promised to another, and other Yürük men are now expected to look upon her as their sister, and to protect her honour if called on to do so. Under no circumstances must they be caught looking at her with desirous eyes, neither must they encourage her to display signs of similar weakness.

A woman who binds her *dalfez* with a coloured scarf is newly married. The same scarf over unplaited hair means she is a wife and mother, no longer interested in the frivolities of flirtation. A widow wears a black silk scarf. If she wishes to remain a widow she leaves her hair unplaited, but if she has in mind another husband she plaits her hair, and is more forthcoming in public.

Marriages are usually arranged by the parents and generally not before the girl is fifteen. But the degree of freedom left to the young girls is wide and I was told that it is not unusual for a young man chosen by the parents to be rejected. Since no betrothal has been formally arranged, and no announcement made, this reflects no shame on the would-be suitor. Sometimes, however, he is so overcome by passion that he attempts to abduct the girl and take her away by force to some other part of the mountains, even down to the plains. This at once leads to violence and bloodshed, often feuding.

A marriageable girl who falls in love with an eligible young man declares her love by setting the dinner table a different way. All the family spoons are placed in the usual manner but her own spoon is reversed, pointing away from her. This means, 'My bread is at another table than yours.' The parents question her and she names the young man.

In like manner, the Yürük man who has set his heart on a wife places another spoon beside his own. This tells his parents: 'I have chosen my wife; I wish her to take her place at this table beside me.' He in his turn is questioned and the father of the girl approached.

Etiquette is strict. A new bride is not expected to speak or do her share of the family work until invited to do so by her parents-in-law. I heard tell of the bride whose in-laws either forgot or overlooked to give their permission, and while her mother-in-law scolded and spoke in her presence about her laziness for not helping with the work, she was forced to sit miserably silent, unable to utter a sound. This went on for sixteen years, by which time her own eldest daughter was getting married. During the celebrations the father-in-law remembered he had never heard his daughter-in-law's voice, and – breaking etiquette – she burst into a sudden torrent of speech and tears and said she had never yet been given permission. From that day to this, however, she hasn't stopped talking, and her mother-in-law died from her scoldings . . .

There is another way in which marriages are arranged, and the origins of this custom are linked with the superstition that is rife among all Yürük people. The father of the girl who has been asked in marriage buys a block of coarse salt which is put in a special corner of the tent and is used in the family cooking. It takes several months for all the salt to be used up, and all the time it is diminishing slowly the poor girl grows feverish with despair, often goes off her food and is so run down that she is in danger of going into a decline. What if, after all the months she has watched this monstrous lump of salt diminishing, her father says no, after all? The thought is too terrible to be borne, and perhaps she takes to her bed with despair.

The father's answer depends on what happens while the salt is in the tent. If everything seems to go well – although even a cut finger can be regarded as a bad omen – his answer will be yes. The signs are propitious; it will be a lucky marriage. Of necessity, much deception takes place. If the mother contracts a stye on her eye or an adolescent son breaks out in pimples, these afflictions are hidden from the father's eagle eye – even if it means that the mother never approaches him in daylight, when he would see at once the eye infection, or the boy has to be sent into the forest until such time as the salt is used up or his pimples disappear.

The girl herself, however, is liable to develop fits of weeping for no apparent reason or become so run down that she has to take to her bed. Her chances are ruined. Her father will refuse to let her marry since her illness happened while the salt was in the tent, and the young man, scared by her wan face and delicate air, will choose another more robust girl.

The status of a man is as easily defined, to those in the know, as that of a woman. All single men, for instance, wear a specially embroidered sock, woven by their mothers from a pattern nearly as old as time itself, and called *kuçuk aǧa'nin çorabi* (the young man's sock). The married man wears a sock woven by his wife to a different design and this is known as *büyük aǧa'nin çorabi* (the married man's sock). These customs are universal among the tribes and no matter where Yürük meet they are recognisable to each other.

There are no schools. The graceful children grow up to complete illiteracy, speaking a pure Turkish that has remained virtually unchanged for ten centuries. The language is monosyllabic. The Yürük do not waste breath, or temper, exploring a sentence for its finer shades; the one exception to this was the shaman who cast his spell on me, and even his language might be said to have been lifted straight from the Koran.

They have no literature or art. Their poetry is inarticulate to the point of meaninglessness, and although there *is* a rough beauty inherent in many of their songs, even when they try to express a yearning they do so with rough, everyday language. They know nothing of architecture, and were virtually untouched by the advent of the Ottoman Empire or by its fall and the rise of the new Turkey. They are still in the ancestral stage and speak of heroes dead a thousand years or more as if they are still alive.

Their silent language, however, is clear in every shade of meaning, a pictorial language older than the one they have learned to speak.

The embroidered socks of the men, the headdresses of the women are symbols of that wordless language. It is there in the interiors of the tents, where every man, woman and child has his seat from the cradle to the grave, and where the rugs placed for guests are never used by anyone else.

The rugs have their symbolic meanings too. The weave and texture are the same, only the motifs are different. These convey exact sentiments, with no explanatory side-tracking. Desire, longing, waiting, disappointment, love, sorrow, joy, circumcision, enmity, friendship – they are all there for the initiated to read. The story of their lives could be written in a sequence of coloured motifs.

Year after year, century after century, the same rugs are woven, the pattern never varying, always requiring precisely the same number of stitches, the same colours. The names they give the rugs are charming, although the names are never used in conversation – only the design itself speaks. There is a rug called 'Golden Slipper' and, strange echo of the Cinderella legend, this is laid beside the hearth to welcome the new bride. There is one called 'The Turtle-Doves Are Angry', and when this is on the floor, no visitor is left in any doubt as to the relations between husband and wife. The rug of 'One Hand and One Place' symbolises true love, and I found it touching, after recognising it, to see this rug displayed in so many of the older people's tents. 'White Cloud' was more obscure, even Osman not knowing the precise meaning, but he thought it was only laid when there was a very small quarrel between a man and his wife, something too trivial to warrant use of 'The Turtle-Doves Are Angry'. 'The Drunken Way' is not a reflection on the drinking habits of the Yürük, who are almost strictly teetotal. Instead, it means that the family within that tent is harassed. Perhaps there are too many mouths to feed, too many difficulties to be faced, not enough money, so that 'The Drunken Way' becomes the symbol of the father's state of mind. When 'The Heart's Hook' is laid it means that a young man has fallen in love and wishes to present his suit to the girl's father. The most commonly seen is 'Laughing Mother', a charming tribute to the patient, hardworking Yürük woman, whose lightness of heart keeps her family happy. 'Running after a Lover' is the remark the neighbours make about a girl ready for marriage, and this rug is left on the floor until the girl is betrothed – always, of course, allowing for odd changes in case of a family quarrel or any other minor calamity. 'The Nest of the Mad One' is a less happy rug, and in the tent where this is displayed a member of the family has either lost his or her mind or a demented lover is nursing his sorrow after rejection by his love. This is a sad black rug, with a wild arabesque of lines running in all directions.

Presents have a language too. The gift of a pink handkerchief means 'I love you', and very often this is the first indication to a young girl that she has a potential lover. A black handkerchief is the gift exchanged between enemies.

They are hidebound by taboos. They have freedom and yet no freedom, for their tribal etiquette is often more frightening than if they lived in chains. The very simplicity of their lives proves shocking after a time. They have no ambition, and the farther away they can climb from the Ankara government the happier they are. They know nothing of democracy, and they fear the *jandarma* who may restrict their wild liberty. Even in summers of great drought, when they are literally face to face with starvation, they have never been known to go down to the farms to work. On the mountains, in their own tents, they are kings.

Their music and their dancing are inherited from Mongolian ancestors; they have added nothing new. Even the songs they sing are handed down from one generation to another. They have never known how to read or write and my gold fountain-pen was a source of endless wonderment to them. They are experts at reproducing Arabic symbols from the Koran but they have never had the wish to invent anything of their own. This, of course, is due to the instability of their lives, since only in a settled society can invention take place. It is also an expression of their natural conservatism.

The adventurous young men who have travelled as far as Konya, and have sometimes been caught by the *jandarma* and sent off to do their army service, return to the tents gladly, shattered by the confinement of barracks and mentally worn out by the abusive officers who seldom have quite such raw material to work on. These young men tell grim tales of the marching, the manoeuvres, the cleaning out of latrines in the officers' quarters, until they assume a sort of epic quality, a dread saga of faraway places where freedom is unknown and where a man is not his own master. The horror is relived each time the story is repeated, and the young man's terrible misfortunes are tales for a long winter evening.

They have no knowledge of their country, or its development. They call themselves 'Yürük', never 'Turk'. The country was theirs originally, they will tell you, taken from them by intruders, who forced them into the mountains.

They are a simple, yet complicated, people, living a way of life that has survived the overthrow of an empire, earthquakes and world disasters. When they die they leave nothing behind them of permanence, save what is permanent in their own customs and their speech. They are one of the few remaining peoples of the world whose own ancestors could recognise them as palpably their own descendants.

Before we left I went out with a hunting party once more, the little mare used to my weight by now, and trained to eat her ration of sugar from my hand. We had grown fond of each other; she would whinny when she saw me and come running to snuffle at my hand, later at my pockets, demanding to be given whatever it was she was sure I had brought her. There were days when she and I rode off together under the vast blue immensity of the sky, where small puffballs of clouds stained the red earth with their moving shadows, sometimes floating so low that they wreathed the distant mountains like snow. This was the good part of Yürük life, this freedom of a man and his horse, riding the wild, bleak countryside, dipping into indigo valleys, resting by the side of a sheltering rock, alone, happy, majestic, the horse cropping the burned grass, raising her head every now and then to look with soft large eyes at her rider, dozing in the shade.

Once I shot a pheasant, a beautiful creature with glinting green collar and reddish tail and markings in black like a fish's backbone. It flew out of a hollow under brambles, its sudden ringing cry taking me by surprise even though I was alert for its appearance, the loud alarmed flapping of its wings synchronising with my shot. Dursun Bey cooked it over a fire that was more smoke than flame. We were unable to judge how long it would take to cook, and once it fell into the fire and we rescued it with difficulty, burning our fingers in the process. Alas, it was tough, and Cemal clucked with annoyance, saying he should never have left the job to me. Tearing at the uneatable flesh, we glared at each other. Too proud to ask our hosts for food, we retired to bed hungry. I reflected, somewhat sadly, on my inability to be a nomad.

There were bears on Karadağ but I only saw one, and I shall never forget it. It remains with me, a touching memory of the free life and a demonstration of the terrible inability of man and beast to communicate.

It was early afternoon when it happened. One of the Yürük women came flying into the camp screaming something I couldn't follow. Osman, who was with us, paled and jumped up, but Hikmet Bey caught him by the arm, asking the reason for his alarm.

'The bear has taken her daughter,' Osman said. 'One of the other children has just told her.' He hurried over to the distraught woman.

I knew about the bear. It lived in a hollow of rock on the far side of the mountain and was known to have at least one cub; its mate had been killed a few weeks before.

The news of the missing child shocked the camp and the few men who were about collected their horses and their guns and rode off. Dursun Bey, Cemal and I joined them. We were all silent, the women gathered into a little distressed knot, comforting the mother of the child and watching our going with anxious eyes. My heart was beating fast and I hoped, if I was called upon to do so, I should be able to acquit myself nobly. There was no doubt that the bear had the child, a girl of three, for her companions had seen her carried off before their eyes and had run, crying, to the mother who was working in the fields.

It was late afternoon before we reached the hollow and we dismounted a short distance away, moving warily. The father and another man, with Cemal and myself immediately behind them, went first, listening for a time outside the lair. There was no noise at all inside and one of the men decided to shine his torch inside. The child was seen sitting on the hard earth, her eyes wide and, as we discovered afterwards, temporarily dumb with shock. There was no sign of the bear but the dead body of the cub lay in a corner close to the child, the smell of its decomposing body already suffocating and quite unbelievably rank. The father picked up the child and carried her outside but I had time to notice that in front of where she had been sitting there were masses of wild pears and a pile of juniper berries. There was no sign of the bear.

I held the child while the father mounted his horse. The few moments she rested in my arms I felt her whole thin little body trembling and once she looked up at me, her eyes wide and dark but quite tearless.

A shout from one of the men waiting a little way down the rocky pass warned us that the bear was coming. It was still some way off, shambling towards us and moving with surprising speed, its arms full of green stuff. The child screeched and turned her face against her father's shoulder and at the sound of her voice the bear stood quite still for a moment, the little eyes darting everywhere. The father moved off with the child but we waited for the bear; since it had already taken a child, it had to be killed. It grunted again, moved forward then fell heavily, killed cleanly by a bullet fired by Cemal which went singing over our heads, making the horses rear up. The men congratulated Cemal, for the shot had entered straight between the eyes.

Riding back to camp, the bear slung between ropes, the men discussed the affair. The child was, apart from almost insane fright, unhurt. Still unable to speak, she could not tell us what had happened. The dead cub indicated that the bear, moved by who knows what savage grief, had taken the child to replace it. That was the conclusion the men came to anyway; the truth could never be known.

We were with the Yürük three weeks, hardly long enough to write about them with authority. We barely scratched the surface.

They were as indifferent to our going as they had been to our arrival. We had made little impression on them; we were scarcely more than a ripple on the surface of their lives. Our struggle to understand them, to make something grand and heroic out of them, linking them to Primitive Man, left them amused, bewildered, perhaps a little disdainful. We remained strangers.

10

The Temperamental Autobüs – Lake Beyşehir –
Antalya – Mersin – Adana – The Professor – Au Revoir

AT MERAM a pile of letters from London awaited me. These I tore open, reading them in no sort of sequence. My wife's letters are always amusing and satisfying and so vividly does she express an idea that I was able to pretend she was beside me – casual, slightly breathless from all the things she still had to tell me, a little inattentive at my own long-windedness. As I bathed, I visualised her large, myopic eyes examining me: together we explored a tooth that was beginning to hurt, we agreed I needed a haircut, but we decided that on the whole I was quite a fine figure. This pleasant reverie was interrupted by Hikmet Bey's exasperated voice telling me that if I didn't hurry up there would be no hot water left for anybody else. I sighed and reached for a towel. She was *not* with me, yet her happy presence was everywhere. Life was so good that I could have climbed a mountain single-handed; it was like being in love all over again.

I was going on to Antalya, Dursun Bey accompanying me, and Hikmet drove us into Konya where we were going to take the *autobüs*. However, the *autobüs* proved recalcitrant from the first. After we had bade our friends goodbye, disposed our luggage unsatisfactorily in the narrow racks and taken our seats, the driver had an argument with an inspector and then walked off in a huff. We watched the inspector spreading his hands regretfully and with emphatic, sympathetic nods through the windows we agreed with this misfortune. Life, we said, was very difficult, but surely there was another driver? Commiserating with our hopes, the inspector shouted that he would do his best. Another driver was hauled from a coffee shop. He stared at the anxious faces pressed against the windows, spat, and announced that under no circumstances would he drive such a bus. He joined the first driver and, reinforced by each other's presence, they heaped abuse on us, on the inspector and the bus company. The inspector ordered us off the bus.

Uproar broke out immediately. An old woman with a basket of grapes said she was on her way to visit her daughter-in-law who had given birth to twins. The birth had been difficult and the woman feared that unless she reached Antalya on time, her daughter-in-law would be dead, and there would be nobody to look after her poor son, God help him, who had never had to do anything for himself in his life. 'Wai, wai, wai,' she wailed, a few synthetic tears rolling down her withered cheeks.

A man in his shirtsleeves bellowed that the devil's luck should seize all drivers and inspectors, and anybody else who dared to obstruct him in his efforts to reach his destination. He was a poor man, he said. He was unable to walk the distance to Eskiköy (a village halfway between Konya and Antalya), and he had spent his last *kuruş* on the dirty *autobüs* which now had no driver. He said if he were able to drive he would take us to Antalya himself, and he looked round at us challengingly and demanded which of us was able to drive. We maintained an uneasy silence. He pummelled the inspector on the chest and said he ought to be shot; it was the likes of him that kept the country poor.

After he had quieted down a bit, we learned why he was in such a bad temper. He had a beautiful daughter, he said, of just seventeen, so beautiful that roses sprang up wherever she walked. A rich landowner, who was ready to give his eyes for her, had asked to marry her and the obstinate girl declared he was too old for her. Her heart, she said, could never burn for *him*. 'Allah!' said the man telling us the story. 'My heart would burn for his money alone!' He and his wife had overruled their ungrateful child and plans had been made to announce the betrothal in two days' time. All the neighbours had been invited. It was going to be the match of all time, and there was the obstinate girl crying herself silly, reddening her eyes and refusing to lift a finger to help her mother. Truly, he said, life was hard for parents. God had given everyone else a child but himself a cucumber . . . So now he was on his way to Eskiköy where there lived a famous *hoca* who made 'heart-binding' spells. The whole world knew how potent his love philtres were, and naturally he charged a lot of money for his services. The father said he had saved for nearly three months, starving himself in the process, going to bed 'on a mouthful of cheese' so that the beautiful daughter would find her rich suitor desirable. However, time was getting short. He had to be back in his own village before dawn the next day, for if the girl wasn't given the potion to drink before dawn it wouldn't be any good. And, God in heaven, who had invented such a dishonourable bus service that took money from the poor and then wouldn't provide a driver . . .

A respectable lawyer from Ankara listened to us with disdain, tchk-tchking while the man talked, eventually moving away from us altogether to the more congenial company of a pretty young woman with two small children, who were on their way to Antalya for a holiday. Ineffably charming, undoubtedly with heart of blackest intent, the lawyer chucked one of the children under the chin.

There had been a number of peasant women in the bus and now they stood about awkwardly, their black shawls drawn tightly across their heads, covering most of their faces. They had baskets of live hens at their feet, and the hens squawked intermittently while their owners huddled together in witchlike conspiracy.

The inspector came back with another driver and we were all herded into the bus again. The peasant women squabbled angrily among themselves because the lawyer had now taken the best seat for himself, the one which had formerly been used to house the crates of hens. The hens were displeased too at the indignity of being set upon the luggage rack, and when I put my bag up my finger was nipped smartly by a Rhode Island

Red, who had managed to thrust nearly half her body through the crate, which at any moment was likely to topple on Dursun Bey's head.

It took some time for the engine to come to life, and the first two drivers came across to call names at the third.

'You'll all be killed,' one of them shouted at us, rapping his knuckles so hard against the windows that I thought he would splinter the glass. 'That bus is a death trap. It should have been taken off the road months ago. You'll never get to Antalya!'

We laughed uneasily, hoping there was no truth in it.

The engine suddenly leaped into life and we rushed forward at a demoniac speed, scattering dogs, venturesome children and the other drivers, who shook their fists after us. Our speed was a temporary matter, however, and before we reached the outskirts of the town we were reduced to a slow crawl and then came to a stop; the driver got down to open the bonnet and tinkered inside for a few minutes. We set off again, the driver now bent over the wheel like a racing fanatic, his face grim with the effort of maintaining any speed at all.

I said I was bored, and would go to sleep.

'Well, you know how it is,' said Dursun Bey, ashamed of the inadequacies of the bus. 'We like to *think* we're up to date, you know.'

'There's no need to apologise to me,' I said. 'I'm not a foreigner.'

Despite all our fears, the bus held together. Now and then it shuddered, the people at the back getting the worst of the vibration, and once, when we rounded a corner at too smart a pace, a crate of hens fell off the rack with a deafening crash, a splintering of rotten wood and uproar from the indignant hens. The lawyer, by this time very friendly with the pretty woman, drew out a cologne stick and rubbed it across her forehead tenderly. Several hens, dazed by their freedom, flew squawking up and down the bus, their eyes rolling in madness and their feathers fluttering all over the place. They were caught with difficulty, and not without injury. With a second finger bitten nearly in half, I was ready to wring their necks.

We stopped again and once more the driver poked about inside the bonnet. This time, however, he lacked the magic touch. We were stranded in the middle of open country.

We all got out to stretch our legs, and the driver said there was a coffee-house a bit farther along the road where he would be able to get help, *provided* the man he wanted, who was a mechanic, was there. If not . . . he shrugged his shoulders and grinned at us darkly and derisively.

'I suppose it will mean waiting for the next bus,' said the lawyer, 'but I shall certainly report this disgraceful service to the proper authorities.' His haughty gaze included us all. He looked the sort of man to whom ministers deferred.

'*Ha sikdir ulan pezevenk!* Complain wherever you like! Your authorities are not giving me my bread. There is no next bus, where do you think you are – in the streets of Ankara!' the driver retorted insolently. 'We load up in Konya.'

'You could always ask a lift from a lorry,' I suggested.

'I should prefer, if it were possible, to hire a car,' said the lawyer distantly, and blew his nose into a large silk handkerchief.

The driver hawked insultingly at the lawyer's feet, then blew his nose with two fingers. 'A car!' he said, and shouted with laughter.

With the exception of the peasant women, we all left our luggage in the bus. The women refused to be parted from their hens and Dursun Bey and I, feeling ungallantly that gallantry was rather being thrust on us, offered to carry the crates, including the broken one which had been patched up insecurely with string.

The road was so poor that it was no wonder the buses broke down from time to time. The driver, talkative now, said that as far as he remembered no servicing was ever carried out on the buses. They came, smart and gleaming, from the factory, then were subjected to a slow but sure murdering on the road. Even allowing for his exaggeration, that was probably near enough to the truth.

I was in no hurry, however. I had no commitments, no appointments to keep. I was prepared to linger here indefinitely. After the aridity of

Karadağ this place was a green enchantment, where every hedgerow was alive with agrimony, rosy pink house-leek and, here and there, the poisonous hemlock, so delicate-looking with its snow-white flowers and feathery leaves. A golden oriole flew out of a thicket, a splash of wonderfully vivid colour against the clear sky. My heart lifted. It was good to be alive. Why worry about the vagaries of transport?

The coffee-house stood in a grove near Lake Beyşehir, a thirty-kilometre expanse of blue water surrounded on all sides by thick forests. As far as I was concerned, the bus could not have broken down at a pleasanter spot. From the top of the hill where we stood we had an uninterrupted view of the lake, shining below like a vast mirror, with the waxy smell of the pine trees scenting the air above us.

Dursun Bey and I bought rye bread, hard-boiled eggs – which the coffee-house keeper obligingly shelled for us – black olives and *turşu*. We set off to the lake. The driver, who was talking with a mild-looking little man who turned out to be the mechanic, shouted after us that he would be ready in an hour or two. We saw him wink at the coffee-house owner as he loped off. We discovered he was going to visit a girlfriend in a village not far away. Being on the road so often, he seldom saw his wife and he had a selection of girlfriends in villages up and down the country.

Down by the lake my old friend the cormorant was fishing intently. We watched him for a while, admiring his dark-blue body, with its bronze-green side wings and the bright splash of white on his under-belly. The blue of lake and sky had the brilliancy and sharpness of enamel. The colour of the water was ever changing – here a vivid cerulean, there the exact shade of a beetle's wing in the sun, darkly green. Farther out, the wind ruffled it to a dark-blue turbulence.

It was a place of birds. The still air quivered with their twitterings and the eye was gladdened by their amazing colours – rosy flame, misty grey, clear emerald green, a brief spark of whirring electric blue – exotic, fanciful, the wings as delicate as gossamer. The most beautiful bird often had the harshest cry but the glittering bright beauty of all of them was compensatory.

'A good place for duck-shooting,' said Dursun Bey.

The whole inner expanse of shining water seethed with duck life – with mallards, eiders and gentle-looking little black tufteds, their innocent white heads bobbing over the gently heaving water.

A bunch of coots wheeled inland, enchanted with the warmth of the day and the cool water beneath them. They whirled overhead, their wings darkening the sun, their wet grey underbellies iridescent. A stiff breeze had blown up, feathering the water with foam, rocking the little black tufteds, and the coots lifted, soared, carried by the wind. Rising far out they whirled down the path of the wind like leaves in an autumn gale, down, down over the whitening water and the green rushes at the lake's edge, wild and free. Two mallards, a drake and a duck, came scudding over after the coots, high and handsome, dark outlines against the summer sky.

We finished our lunch, scattering crumbs for the exotic birds who were too shy to take them.

Back at the coffee-house there was no sign of the driver. The mechanic, who had carried out some sort of running repairs to the bus, pored over an out-of-date American magazine which showed pictures of racing cars. He could not read the text; the pictures satisfied him. He said it was his ambition to own a racing car. We were all a little weary by the time the driver appeared, his swagger and his bold smile of satisfaction indicating that he had been successful in the village.

Antalya, seen against a flaming sunset, never disappoints. It is at this time of the day that the neglected gardens become mysterious and secretive. The half-circle of houses assumes a romantic air. The city walls rise sharply above rambling fig trees, the wild pear and plane trees that seem nearly as tall as the cliffs themselves.

A café, wreathed in vines, served us freshly caught fish and a local red wine which had unfortunately been iced. The proprietor said he could let us have a room for the night, but unless we were willing to pay for the four beds it held, he couldn't guarantee a quiet night. I think Dursun Bey would have been agreeable to taking the risk, but I was adamant and we paid for all the beds.

After eating, we went down to the harbour. The houses here are smothered in wistaria, the scent overpowering, the beauty sharp, lush and dramatic. The red earth above the harbour is thick with trees, tangled bushes and weeds grow knee high. It is a haven of peace, and here amid a grove of silver birch, we sat down facing the bay. The peaks of Çalbalidağ soared up, tier after amber-coloured tier, woody green and olive green, clothed in a forest of leaves, as majestic as a queen, the sea sweeping its feet. Houses ran down to the edge of the water, where rowing boats bobbed up and down gently. Old walls were covered with creeper, with vines and with the bold wistaria. There was a smell of salt and seaweed.

As the sun sank lower, the breeze died down and the confined water of the bay became still as green glass, a mirror reflecting a sky from which all colour had fled. Even the sun itself, sinking on the horizon, was a blanched glare of fierce light without hue. The great expanse of water, with the sails of fishing boats reflected darkly, became mysterious and urgent, silent but for the soft splash of waves against the shore. The light changed subtly, became clearer and deeper. From a coffee-house somewhere behind us a radio played peasant music, but at this distance the singer's voice was barely audible. The rhythmic thrumming of the *ud*, and the high notes of the violin reached us in little eddying waves of sound, fading, dying, brought to life again. I was reminded of Karadağ and the Yürük people and a terrible nostalgia gripped me.

A gull alighted quite near us, its blood-red bill sharp as a razor-blade, the chocolate-brown head tipped sideways, alert to the slightest movement we made. In the extraordinary clarity of the evening, its body looked pure white. After a time it flew seawards, into the face of the dying sun, and following its flight we had to screw up our eyes against the glare on the horizon.

The day died, the sky arching high, the water darkening coldly. Dusk enfolded us and presently the stars came out one by one, reflected in the rippling waters of the bay like drops of quicksilver. Seascape and landscape blended. A ship's siren echoed across the harbour, sounding a note of melancholy.

I realised suddenly that destination had no meaning for me. There was no point of arrival. I had assumed the guise of traveller, chained for a brief moment *here* but anxious to be off *there*, where distance, perhaps legend, held new enchantment. Like the Turks themselves, wanderers through the centuries from the time they left their home beyond the Tien Shan hills, I had nowhere to call home. They were strangers who pitched their tents where the land was most fertile.

We returned late to the city, walking through the vast public gardens where creepers covered the nudity of statues, sometimes climbing in such a way, and from such an angle, that they hid only the private parts of the alabaster figures, looking for all the world like some gigantic outcrop of pubic hair. Dursun Bey left next day, and I was alone again.

In his famous book of travels, Ibn Battuta writes of Antalya's apricots; I was reminded of this as I lay supine in a *hamam*, breathless after the untender ministrations of a masseur, when a youth, no doubt in an attempt to revive me, brought me a dish of them. It was sacrilege to eat them. They were firm and red, and larger than the largest peaches I have ever seen. To bite into their deep orange flesh was to taste the nectar of the gods.

After such apricots one expects anything, and one is right, for the climate of Antalya is kind, the land fertile. Whatever fruits one desires are found there, and indeed on a monument dedicated to Hadrian, carved in bas-relief, are pomegranates, oranges, lemons, figs, dates and every other fruit ever grown. Even in the most neglected gardens there are orange trees, and the honey melons rival those of the eastern region, watered by the Euphrates.

The town is on the crest of prosperity and in the harbour the boats load grain, rice, fruits and bales of cotton.

I spent a good deal of my days at the harbour. Time was forgotten while I leaned over the moss-covered wall, hypnotised by the rise and fall of the quiet water. Rowing-boats plied between the cargo-boats, the oarsmen brown as mahogany, their white teeth flashing as they cursed each other good-naturedly. At nightfall other brown-skinned men put out for the night's catch, the lanterns winking like great eyes from the prows of their old-fashioned boats. During the day they sat along the harbour wall mending their nets, exchanging gossip and abuse and ogling the women. Their ramshackle houses lined the waterfront, the sea almost lapping their front doors.

There are flowers everywhere; I think these are the memories one retains of Antalya – the sweet-smelling wild flowers, the trees and the quiet sea. Even the woody valleys blaze with oleanders and rhododendrons. Roses grow well and once there was a city called Rhodiopolis from which rose perfume was exported to Greece, and it became a fashion among the ladies of Athens to boast that they used nothing else but the scents from Rhodiopolis. Ornaments made of lemon wood were also exported and in the markets of Rome they fetched more than Africa's ivory.

I tore myself away eventually, going on to Mersin by boat. We sailed close inshore in the dew-filled morning and details of rocks and trees glistened as though painted on canvas. The world was hazy with autumn. At early evening, mists wreathed the trees so that they seemed to float in the air, rootless. Leaning over the boat's rail that morning, I watched the receding hills grow less and less substantial as they climbed into a colourless sky. On the shore road an ox-cart, laden with sweet red peppers, lumbered into market, dwarfed by the background of mountains, where groves of olives encroached on the young green beeches like clouds of smoke.

My travelling companions were few and had as little merit about them as I had myself. We had twenty-eight hours in which to get to know each other, but in those first moments we showed no desire to do anything else but glower at each other morosely, intent on keeping ourselves to ourselves at all costs.

The landscape grew wilder and emptier, and for a time there was only the open sea and the pale line of the pine forests to our left. The water was as still as glass, reflecting our pristine whiteness as faithfully as a mirror. By dinner that evening some of the passengers had thawed sufficiently to call for a *tric-trac* set. Two army officers and a naval doctor invited me to play poker, one of the army officers looking disconcerted when I won the stakes, which were high. Selfishly, I refused to continue to play and for the remainder of the night they avoided me; my stock was low. I weakened after lunch the next day, however, and they had their revenge, but since I had cunningly called for lower stakes they didn't clean me out completely. We parted friends.

Mersin emerged in afternoon sunlight, lying on a green plain and backed by the immense snow-tipped heights of the Taurus Mountains. Men were selling baskets of freshly pulled oranges on the quayside. A new harbour has been built, with warehouses looking like vast white cubes. The products of the great Cilician Plain are handled here – the timber, fruits, cotton and grain which are shipped to Syria and Russia.

I found I had three hours to wait for the Adana train, and after I had eaten I hired a horse-drawn carriage to take me round the town. The roads, newly constructed, were excellent until we had gone a kilometre or so outside Mersin and then they deteriorated into mere tracks. Camels plodded along, burdened with bales of cotton, taking up nearly all the road so that we were forced to retreat into the leafy ditches. Behind the camels was a sleek American car, driven by a hawk-faced man with a silk scarf knotted round his neck. The driver of the carriage saluted him respectfully and told me he was the owner of the camels. Besides this he owned a good deal of property in and around Mersin. Two of his sons were being educated in America and a third was a prosperous doctor in Istanbul.

Mersin in sunlight is picturesque, with vine-wreathed cafés and ramshackle wooden houses shaded by plane trees. In bad weather, however, the side-streets must be veritable seas of mud. Along the waterfront there is the usual rash of new villas, sparklingly white and prosperous-looking in well-laid-out gardens. In the public park, the low-growing palms fight a continual battle with the salt-laden air.

The Ankara government plans to make Mersin the leading port in Southern Turkey and, like all pseudo-cities in a state of transition, it is in that unpleasant halfway stage between demolition and reconstruction. Nevertheless, there is a certain spurious charm about the place.

The malarial swamps have been cleaned up and groves of citrus fruits planted on the outskirts of the town. There is a good drainage system and land reclaimed from the swamps is well irrigated. The people themselves radiate solidity and cheerfulness and talk of little else beside the great plans Ankara have in store for them. I was not sorry to leave them to their hopes and go on to Adana.

The town of Adana, the third largest in Turkey, is prosperous but colourless. There are plenty of cotton millionaires but they are less ostentatious than their forefathers, and in place of the palaces the Ottomans might have built there are only the showy white villas, with a monotony of red roofs, and a bleak-looking mosque in the modern manner. Wealth has not yet bred culture and the money brought in by cotton is lodged safely in the banks.

One or two new hotels have been built – all marble and chrome on the outside, with washbasins in every room – and they charge exorbitant prices. There are a few textile factories, a Cotton Institute, where farmers can exchange their old seed for new or buy the new seed at reduced prices, and a model cotton farm where expert advice is available free to any peasant who cares to make use of the service.

Adana's younger generation, the sons and daughters for the most part of rich fathers, are educated in America; rarely nowadays in Germany. They all speak English with a pronounced American accent. They have a passion for jazz records, and even rock 'n' roll is not unknown in this remote corner of Asia Minor. A few of them are brave enough to appear in public in check over-shirts and jeans. They drive fast, brightly coloured sports cars and have a liking for Coca-Cola.

The contrast between old and new is apparent even on the wide new boulevard, where sleek American cars toot impatiently behind a string of slow-moving camels or ox-carts with iron-rimmed wheels. In the public gardens there is the inevitable statue of Kemal Atatürk, looking stern. The whole place seethes with Americans; it was they who built the aerodrome. They invade the cafés by night, where their favourite steak and eggs is always on call.

The shops are full of gold watches, refrigerators, radiograms, washing machines and high-priced cars – the infallible barometers of a city's wealth. Peasants from across the great Plain, horsemen from the Taurus Mountains come to Adana in fascinated awe, perhaps feeling that here in this boom-town they are in touch with the greater world beyond their own frontiers. Bright red tractors are displayed in the windows of a new emporium, and on Saturday nights the roads leading to the dance-halls and nightspots are crowded with tractors, driven in by the farmers' sons who have no car. Newly rich peasants house their tractors, symbols of their prosperity, in specially erected shacks where a member of the family stands night-guard lest envious neighbours despoil the new toy. The tractors are decorated with blue beads to ward off the Evil Eye, just as were the camels in the recent past.

My host in Adana was my old professor of German in Kuleli Military Academy. He spent his days pottering about a huge weedy garden in old felt slippers and writing a history of the Turks to which he had already devoted ten years of research. His house was a low-lying white *konak*, still lit by oil lamps, with damp and mildew encroaching rapidly in the empty rooms. His *salon* was his bedroom, his kitchen and his library. It was filled with oddments of furniture taken from the other rooms. Books were stacked on roughly made shelves, on tables that sometimes sagged from their weight, and on the floor where they mouldered in dusty piles. For company he had a nearly blind dog, who followed him everywhere, and an old moulting parrot who was rude to strangers. The parrot and I disliked each other on sight. Cocking its head on one side, it regarded me evilly, then swore. I returned the insult and it battered madly against the bars of its cage, obviously longing to peck my eyes out.

The professor, a charming eccentric, did all his own marketing, carrying a large string bag from which purchases kept escaping so that he left a trail behind him wherever he went. This trait was well known in the district and children were always turning up at the house with things like reels of cotton, minute packages of tea, three or four withered potatoes and so on, certain not only of their five *kuruş* tip but of the fact that these objects belonged to none other than the professor. The first morning I went marketing with him he lost half a kilo of meat and a packet of small pearl buttons.

He was a fine cook, and since cooking is my own pet fad, I picked up many a culinary tip from him, as well as some out-of-the-way recipes. Unfortunately we were both headstrong and opinionated, neither wishing to retreat an inch from his stated method; over a plate of burned chops, we would reproach each other bitterly, each blaming the other for the fiasco. Peering at me over the rims of his spectacles, pursing his lips anxiously, he would watch while I prepared *şiş kebab*. Each cube of meat was subjected to the intensest examination to see if it had been pounded thinly enough, with every fibre separated. The quantity of herbs I used, the length of time the meat had to marinate in onion juice or wine, were of the greatest possible importance. The *salon* used to stink of cooking, of the unwashed dog and the parrot's droppings. The noise was generally shocking – the professor loudly calling me names, the dog barking approvingly and the parrot, anxious not to be overlooked, adding his own disgusting invective.

We had our quiet moments, of course – when we sunbathed in the garden, for instance, the old dog at our feet hunting for fleas in his mangy coat and snapping at flies he could hear but not see.

I asked the professor what he thought of the new Adana. Pushing up the spectacles on his thin nose and setting aside the nightshirt he was mending, he replied: 'It's a phase which will pass. Every nation has its infantile moments.'

I asked if he did not regret the old days but he considered this a stupid question. Still seeing me as his student, he began to lecture me. He bade me remember that life is progress, that stagnation is death, that the culture of no country can ever be said to die but is carried on by other generations in a different form, yet a form which can be logically traced back to the parent stem. In support of this he cited the Hittite civil laws which, nearly five thousand years ago, set out the prices to be charged for farm animals or the hire of a team of oxen; their penal code laid down punishments for misuse of land tenure and for the non-return of lost property to its rightful owner, and that fees be charged for instructing an apprentice. All these rulings are still valid, recognisable evolution of primitive beginnings.

He spoke of the present-day Turkish peasant who sows a few acres of cotton and becomes rich, perhaps even a millionaire, in less than a decade. 'This is good for the peasant and good for the country,' he said. 'The nation is a living thing, however crude. Each generation imposes its own values, which most likely will not agree with the ones that went before, although a historian will be able to recognise their affinity. All the time there is *movement*, an impetus to do better than one's forefathers, a feeling of being in the swim. Man is a gregarious animal. He likes to be one of a community; he is at his greatest as one of a community. This is the truth underlying Communism.'

I mentioned the Americans, diffidently.

'Once upon a time,' he said, 'it was the classical Greeks, now it's the Americans. It's all one really – only the culture seems different, yet even that is basically the same – the spread of ideals, the betterment of people, the clamour for power. Read your history. It's all there. Only the century is different.'

He viewed life from some Olympian heights of his own, enviably detached – a tatty, untidy old man who censured my admiration of the past as nothing but sentimentality.

He told me of the Tyrrhenians, who had once inhabited Asia Minor, spreading their culture from the vicinity of Troy a millennium before the Christian era. Their most striking characteristic seems to have been their inability to delude themselves about anything, however disagreeable. Effeminate in appearance, inflexibly just, they regarded life with exactitude, as an opportunity only given once, to be seized and used to the full. As a consequence they were grossly sensual and pleasure loving. Unlike many other peoples of antiquity, they thought of the world of the dead as a place of mourning, where the spirits of the departed sorrowed because they could no longer participate in life. This belief gave the pattern to their behaviour; if annihilation was their ending, then at least they would not delude themselves concerning their fate. Since it was impossible to avenge themselves on the gods who had laid the sentence of death on mankind, they vented their wrath on the helpless creatures of these gods. They rejected illusion, and their nihilistic hatred and desperation was their crowning insult to the One who had made them mortal.

The professor accepted their logic and their cruelty. 'For who,' he asked, 'will not be cruel and sensual if he accepts death as the ending of all things?'

He himself seemed to me to be as at home in the past as he was in the present. He regarded the new neon-lighted cinema to be as much a part of history and the century's culture as the Temple of Artemis at Efes; to him they were only facets of the same thing – the march of civilisation and man's urge to create.

When I left for Bursa, he and his dog accompanied me to the airport. His leonine head – the wispy grey hairs blowing in the wind and his glasses slipping down his nose – was the last things I saw as the silver plane soared into an autumn sky, carrying me to Bursa and the first stage of my long journey home.

Afterword

'[Irfan Orga] has imagination, a sense of beauty, a philosophic disposition.
Above all he seeks the truth.'   LORD KINROSS

ENGLAND, a Turkish officer, the glory and the doom. July 1942,
three-year posting. Fighter-pilot. My father finds love. An Air Force
staff captain 'living with a foreign woman' loses a career. Christmas 1947,
one-month visa. Fugitive. Father's liaison 'being established as fact', the
Ministry of National Defence in Ankara petition at his subsequent trial
in absentia (1949), 'he [is] considered as having resigned [his commission, effective from 15 January 1946, and is] dismissed'. Trading affluence
and epaulettes in Turkey for the barest of existences with mother and me
in London (she a Norman-Irish girl from County Wicklow), he left his
land with a price on his head, never to go back. He tried for jobs –
hospital porter, relief postman, whatever he could find. But no one
offered him anything. So he turned to writing, publishing nine books.
The first was *Portrait of a Turkish Family*, a volume of memoirs
(Gollancz); the seventh, *The Caravan Moves On* (Secker & Warburg).
Products of exile, they took shape in the rented tenement lands of post-

war west London – *Portrait* (1949–50) in a cramped, unattractive fourth-floor room at 35 Inverness Terrace, Bayswater, a Greek boarding house; *The Caravan* (1957–8) in a large top-floor one at 7 Pembridge Square, Notting Hill: lighter, airier accomodation, run by a corpulent travel agent.

The difference of environment, the one yellowed and run-down, the other pastel and gentile, was palpable. Historically, Inverness Terrace (Lillie Langtry country) had always been *risqué*, Pembridge Square (old campaigners come home to pasture) retiring. Pembridge Square was up-market, its grand Victorian houses post-dating the 1851 Exhibition. Ramsay MacDonald (who married into the square in 1896) wrote of the 'calm dignity of pillared porticoes, bow-windows, broad steps and massive front doors', of 'that air of detached independence which surrounds the English middle-class home of substantial possessions'. Who previously lived at No. 7 we never knew – in our time it was peopled mainly by spinsters, divorcees and widows, the 1955 Electoral Register showing thirty-one lodgers including my parents. Every now and again, though, there seemed to be the echo, the presence, occasionally even the evidence, of long-silent nurseries, connecting doors, playrooms. For thirty-odd years it had belonged to a Spanish merchant, Ricardo Quintana, the household, according to the 1871 Census, maintaining six servants: a cook, (Spanish) butler, lady's maid, housemaid, footman and kitchen maid. In 1912 it was the address of an Amy Frances, one Mrs Sidney Samuel Jacobsohn, then in her early twenties. Bound second-class for Montreal out of Southampton, she survived the sinking of the *Titanic* – Lifeboat 12. Her husband did not. Pembridge Square was characterful, elegant and comfortable with, to the south-facing back, the leafy invitation of a many-branched tree, full of dappled bowers and watchful owls. To the front, flowering cherries, their glory as brief as a wedding day, would veil the spring pavements in petal-storms of rose-white and coffee-cream.

From Pembridge Square, father and I would set out across Kensington Gardens, past gaggles of starched nannies parading their prams like so many ships-of-the-line. We'd walk along Kensington Palace Gardens, past the dark hammer-and-sickled fortress of the Soviet Embassy, heavily policed following the Hungarian Uprising of 1956. We'd stroll down Kensington Church Street, past No. 128, originally 1 High Row, Kensington Gravel Pits – home to the composer Clementi. Here young Mendelssohn from Berlin would visit the Horsley girls, taking time to sketch the house. Here, following my father's death, I would go for civilised dinners with Tom Stacey, playing Mozart duets and Field nocturnes to tremble the ghosts.

Socially, the high end of the Pembridge vicinity was Addison Road, Campden Hill, the imposing residencies of Holland Park and the park itself (in 1958 a magical wilderness for a boy to play in) together with the reminders of what once had been – the bombed-out shell of Holland House. St Petersburgh Place and its synagogue, near the Greek Orthodox Church in Moscow Road, drew my father. Maybe its walled and iron-latticed gardens and appealingly-painted, plant-festooned houses reminded him of Istanbul's backwaters. The low end was Ladbroke Grove and Portobello Road. Here the barrow boys of the fruit and vegetable market shouted their produce in cries as piercing and unsynchronised as the calls of the muezzin between Aya Sofia and Sultan Ahmet. Live chickens could be had for fresh slaughter. On Saturdays, the antique dealers would take over, haggling and over-pricing themselves in the time-honoured manner of their kind. My father never bought anything. I did occasionally. On Sundays, the market came to the square, hot summer mornings enticing out the strawberry sellers; father always gave mother strawberries on her birthday. The low end reminded us of the fragility of our gentrified existence. Sometimes, it seemed, just a street divided dereliction and poverty from diamonds and prettiness.

Our time in Notting Hill, backdrop to *The Caravan*, was before the area was redeveloped. We had an understanding landlord, happy to claim (even boast) a writer as one of his tenants. Others were not so fortunate. A royal borough North Kensingon may have been, but these were the blackmailing Rachman years. With neo-Edwardian 'Coshers' taunting the Caribbean influx, and gangs of quiffed, side-burned, flick-knifing 'Teds' deterring us from crossing even the short distance to the newly opened public library at No. 1, my father – Rumelian complexion and blue eyes notwithstanding (his womenfolk came from the Balkans) – felt threatened in his foreignness, hampered by his fractured accent. Weekends were for staying at home . . .

. . . and reaching for new horizons. Midsummer Day 1957 my mother went into publishing, joining Martin Secker & Warburg. Suddenly we found ourselves thrown into parties. My father, to his linguistic discomfort, was the centre of attention, an exotic Turk of Ottoman childhood and Republican making, surrounded by a welcoming if curious London literary set. Animated exchanges with the parliamentarian Richard Crossman, conversations with Eric Newby (he who knew the world from Cape Horn to Nuristan), all seem like yesterday. I was thirteen. We returned the hospitality in our own style, bottles of Turkish wine and delicacies from Soho complementing my father's latest culinary triumphs. The charmed, brilliant Peterkiewiczs, Jerzy and Christine (Brooke-Rose), came to Pembridge Square. Lord Kinross (Patrick Balfour) too – later, in 1959, approaching my father to provide the translations and Turkish source material for *Atatürk: The Rebirth of a Nation* (1964). And, of course, the Warburgs – gravel-voiced, equine Fred, Jewish intellectual, living proof that publishing was indeed 'an occupation for gentlemen'.

Seckers were the publishers of Mann, Orwell, Kafka, Gide, Moravia, Barzun, Colette, Angus Wilson, Malraux. To be on their list was to keep the company of the century. But there were drawbacks. In 1958, my father sensed that Eric Newby – more accurately his book *A Short Walk in the Hindu Kush* – was being promoted at the expense of *The Caravan*. His quarrel wasn't with Eric though: he appreciated an autographed copy of *A Short Walk* on his birthday that year, his fiftieth.

If Seckers frustrated him, the critics did not. From *Portrait* to *Atatürk* (1962), the grandees of the establishment celebrated father's work. Harold Nicolson, John Betjeman, Cyril Connolly. *The Caravan* attracted seasoned Turcophiles. Kinross was adamant. My father, he claimed in the *Daily Telegraph*, illuminated Turkey, 'both to the Turk and to the foreigner, as only a sensitive Turkish writer can do. He has all the attributes of the ideal traveller.' In the *Observer*, Freya Stark savoured the 'nomad' chapters. 'In the passing of the days, and the study of [Yürük] customs, the hierarchy of the tents ("every corner [. . .] has its own language"), the legends of their life, and the comparative freedom of their women,' she believed, 'the best chapters of the book are written. The mountain air pervades it, the sun heeling westward from high spaces, "pouring a storm of light over the countryside [. . .] the smell of thyme [. . .] everywhere".'

Final assurance of *The Caravan*'s status came in a letter from Fred (2 September 1958), confirming its selection by the Book Society as one of their forthcoming recommendations – an accolade, 'my dear Irfan', of 'prestige importance.' Despite a German translation in 1960 (Carl Hanser Verlag, Munich), sales were to be disappointing, however. New York rejected it, Cass Canfield of Harper & Brothers reasoning that while it was 'fascinating' and 'vivid', 'there are not enough people in the US concerned with the subject to warrant the hope that we could sell the book successfully' (3 September 1959).

The Caravan was a corporate enterprise – its journey and autobiography my father's, its prose my mother's, its index and endpaper maps mine. To English speakers, *the* Anatolian travellers of the fifties were Stark and Kinross – cultured writers, romantic observers, pre-eminent classicists. Their books were central to the family collection. Superficially, *The Caravan* was of the same cut, down even to occasional similarities of expressive language and imagery. Fundamentally, it was very different. Stark and Kinross were informed antiquarians, my father an instinctive anthropologist. They understood the Turk, his mentality and manner, from without, poetically, he from within, physically. Their culture was imperial British, his oriental Turkish. As an observer, a storyteller amongst his own people, his was the lyric tradition of Evliya Çelebi, theirs the reportage of Richard Chandler and the eighteenth century. Through paperbacks and newspapers sent by his brother, my father was familiar with the Turkish 'pastoral' movement of the early fifties: well-thumbed copies of Mahmut Makal and Yaşar Kemal were always on the table, along with Reşat Nuri. Mother, too, valued Makal, in 1957 paying eighteen shillings (ninety pence) for Wyndham Deedes's translation of *A Village in Anatolia*. Imaginatively, *The Caravan* belonged within this rural literature. But it was more sophisticated, it exchanged peasants for nomads, it lent its diary scenes the veneer of visual documentary.

'Yürük: nomadic or pastoral Turkmen', wanderers of the land, watchmen of the old caravan routes. Community: 320,000 scattered, around 0.5% of Turkey's total population' (Patrick Johnstone, *Operation World*, 1993). Language: a dialect of Balkan Gagauz Turkish (Balkan Turkic), spoken also in Macedonia. Freya Stark depicted them as 'cheerful and fierce', making 'insecurity [their] refuge' (*The Lycian Shore*, 1956). Chandler (*Travels in Asia Minor*, 1775) cameoed 'numerous caravans, chiefly of mules' around the ruins of Lydian Sardis, the 'large and fierce dogs [of the Turcomans] barking vehemently'. Nomads and caravans, dogs and pack animals, their sound and smell, define southern Turkey as much as the landscape, the dust and heat. An American friend, Crawford H. Greenewalt Jr, Director of Excavations at Sardis, remembers that 'in the late 1950s there were still regular camel caravans on the Ankara–Izmir highway, and we saw them – daily? – at Sardis; also at a camel stop in one of the villages between Turgutlu and Izmir.' In Lycia, 'a small [nomadic] camel procession, the camels piled with exotic textiles – rugs and tents – ' once caught his eye.

Trekking the High Taurus, my father ventured powerfully into the mind and midst of the Yürük, first crossing their path in Konya. But when? During service in Izmir in the late 1930s? Following the end of the Second World War, stationed in Kurdish Diyabakir on the Silk Road east? In 1955/6, the date claimed in the original preface (omitted from the present marginally abridged edition)? I have no idea – only that it cannot have been 1955/6, for then he was near penniless in London. ('We have no money,' my mother informed the prime minister, Adnan Menderes, 21 August 1956, 'a writer [. . .] is rich only in spirit'.) Maybe it was felt that such a fiction, together with minor accommodations of narrative, was necessary to give *The Caravan* commercial immediacy. At whose instigation – father's, Fred Warburg's? The question must remain open. No matter. For this is a story beyond the calendars of man, a tale of a 'wild, free' earth people, 'touched with mystery', living their rituals by the round of the seasons beneath the star trails of eternity.

Ateş Orga
Blaxhall, Suffolk
1 May 2002

ELAND

61 Exmouth Market, London EC1R 4QL
Fax: 0207 833 4434
Email: info@travelbooks.co.uk

Eland was started in 1982 to revive great travel books that had fallen out of print. Although the list has diversified into biography and fiction, it is united by a quest for the defining spirit of place. These are books for travellers, readers who aspire to explore the world but who are also content to travel in their mind. Eland books open out our understanding of other cultures, interpret the unknown, reveal different environments as well as celebrating the humour and occasional horrors of travel.

All our books are printed on fine, pliable, cream-coloured paper. They are still gathered in sections by our printer and sewn as well as glued, almost unheard of for a paperback book these days. This gives larger margins in the gutter, as well as making the books stronger.

We take immense trouble to select only the most readable booksand therefore many readers collect the entire series. If you haven't liked an Eland title, please send it back to us saying why you disliked it and we will refund the purchase price.

You will find a very brief description of all our books on the following page. Extracts from each and every one of them can be read on our website, at www.travelbooks.co.uk. If you would like a free copy of our detailed catalogue, please write to us at the above address.

ELAND

'A gold-mine for the discriminating reader' PUBLISHING NEWS

Memoirs of a Bengal Civilian
JOHN BEAMES
A District Officer in India just after the Mutiny

A Visit to Don Otavio
SYBILLE BEDFORD
The Hell of travel and the Eden of arrival in post-war Mexico

The Devil Drives
FAWN BRODIE
Biography of Sir Richard Burton, explorer, linguist and pornographer

My Early Life
WINSTON CHURCHILL
From North-West Frontier to Boer War by the age of twenty-five

A Square of Sky
JANINA DAVID
A Jewish childhood in the Warsaw Ghetto and hiding from the Nazis

Chantemesle
ROBIN FEDDEN
A lyrical evocation of childhood in Normandy

Viva Mexico!
CHARLES FLANDREAU
A journey amongst the Mexican people

Travels with Myself and Another
MARTHA GELLHORN
Five journeys from hell by a great war correspondent

The Weather in Africa
MARTHA GELLHORN
Three novellas set among the white settlers of East Africa

Walled Gardens
ANNABEL GOFF
An Anglo-Irish childhood

A State of Fear
ANDREW GRAHAM-YOOLL
A journalist witnesses Argentina's nightmare in the 1970s

Warriors
GERALD HANLEY
Life and death among the Somalis

Morocco That Was
WALTER HARRIS
All the cruelty, fascination and humour of a pre-modern kingdom

Far Away and Long Ago
W. H. HUDSON
A childhood in Argentina

Holding On
MERVYN JONES
One family and one street in London's East End: 1880–1960

Three Came Home
AGNES KEITH
A mother's ordeal in a Japanese prison camp

Peking Story
DAVID KIDD
The ruin of an ancient Mandarin family under the new Communist order

Scum of the Earth
ARTHUR KOESTLER
Koestler's personal experience of France in World War II

A Dragon Apparent
NORMAN LEWIS
Cambodia, Laos and Vietnam on the eve of war

Golden Earth
NORMAN LEWIS
Travels in Burma